Three Labs a Lifetime

Christopher Morin

Memoirs of the family dog(s) by

CHRISTOPHER W. MORIN

THREE LABS A LIFETIME
Memoirs of the family dog(s)

©2016 Christopher W. Morin

ISBN: 978-1-940244-84-6

designed and produced by
Indie Author Warehouse
Thomaston, Maine
www.indieauthorwarehouse.com

Printed in the United States of America

For my mother, whose love for Mandy, Trucker, and Dillon can only be matched by the unprecedented amount of time, care, and maternal devotion she dedicated to them for thirty-six years of her life.

AUTHOR'S NOTE

In creating this memoir, I made every attempt to be as accurate as possible with the information imparted. The stories, recollections, and dates have all been mined from my memory and personal experiences, as well as discussions with my parents. How I remember a certain event or conversation as it relates to the dogs may not be the way another person present at that time remembers it. Certain thoughts and recollections retold in this narrative are my own personal opinions and speculations that may differ slightly from those of other friends and family members.

CONTENTS

♦ ♦ ♦

"If I were to die today and could come back tomorrow as anything or anybody, I would want to come back as Jane Morin's dog."

—BURKE WALDRON

CHAPTER ONE

MANDY

I honestly don't remember much from my first meeting with the little black canine that would become my family's first dog. My first recollection of a family pet was a black cat we owned named Sam. Sam was my friend. Although we were acquainted for just a very short time—I was only two to three years of age—I do remember petting Sam's glossy, obsidian-colored coat and occasionally chasing him around the house. Sam used to lie on my parents unmade bed all curled up in a tight ball fast asleep. My mother, not wanting to disturb the cat, or perhaps just for fun, used to make Sam right into the bed. I remember being fascinated by the lump under the covers that didn't move an inch until it was good and ready.

My last memory of Sam came from my father, who sat my older brother and I down one day to try and explain why Sam was no longer in the house. He told us that Sam had gotten sick and had to spend some time at the vet. He went on to say that the vet was unable to make him feel better because he had a disease that was incurable. That was the first time I had ever heard of cancer, and the last time Sam was ever mentioned. Fortunately, I have both memories and pictures of that foolish black feline.

My mother was a "cat person." In a world where we often define and categorize individuals as either "cat people" or "dog people," my mother was most definitely a "cat person." Growing up, her family never owned a dog, as my maternal grandmother simply preferred the companionship of cats. That side of the family's preference for feline pets continued all the way up to Sam, who was my parents' first joint pet after they married in 1967.

My father did have one childhood dog named Sporty who was of questionable pedigree. In simpler language, Sporty was a mutt. Later in my father's college years, my paternal grandmother acquired a Dachshund whom she named Fritzy. He lived only a few years, and I have no memory of him except from what I've seen in old photographs and in grainy home movies on decaying 8mm film. So it's safe to say that my father did have more exposure to dogs growing up, but certainly nothing that would prepare him—and my mother—for what was to come in the late summer of 1978.

I was four years old and freshly over one of the worst cases of chicken pox a child could have endured when Mandy first arrived. Sam was gone, and a friend of my mother's decided that the "pet-less" Morin family—more specifically the two little boys—needed a dog. So one day, completely by surprise, my mother's friend Kathy Waldron showed up on my family's doorstep with a little black puppy. As I previously mentioned, I have little to no memory of this first encounter, though my parents have told me of my initial joy at seeing the timid, little black ink spot on four legs, and the excitement I experienced that only a puppy could generate in the eyes of a young boy. There are also pictures of my brother and I cradling Mandy together on the front steps of our house just a few weeks later. This was the beginning of a life-changing experience for my entire nuclear family.

The name "Mandy" was the suggestion of Kathy Waldron. It just seemed right and the name stuck. Mandy was part of a litter of puppies that were being sold off the back of a pickup truck in the parking lot of the Northgate Shopping Plaza in my hometown of Portland, Maine. I'm told a whopping five dollars was the price she fetched! After the cold, hard cash was exchanged, she was plucked out of her box, and in no time she had a new home at 53 Lester Drive in the suburban North Deering section of Portland.

Mandy was a mutt, and the exact pedigrees of her parents are a mystery. Clearly, the dominant breed in her genetic makeup was Labrador retriever, and my family always referred to her simply as a "black Lab" whenever asked. However, it was generally accepted and acknowledged that she was also part sheepdog. Unlike most purebred black Labs, which typically have short hair, Mandy's coat was long and very scruffy. I always claimed that it was the sheepdog genes in her that were responsible for this. Mandy was completely black except for a tuft of white on her chest, lower underside, and a few sprigs of white hairs at the tip of her tail. As an adult dog, she was not exceptionally large in size, but neither was she what I would consider puny. She was feisty and very full of life, which I will detail a bit more later.

For the first eleven-plus years of my life, my family lived on a quiet dead-end street in the suburbs of Portland called Lester Drive. Nine houses lined up in a row on one side of the street faced nine houses lined up on the other side. My family moved there in 1972, and number 53 was my parents' first house. There were thick woods on three sides of the little community that would provide an ideal setting for ample playtime adventures as I grew from infancy into childhood.

There were many young families like mine that lived on Lester Drive at the time. It was a time very different from now. Everybody knew their neighbors, and families were much more social and outgoing than they are today. It was routine to hear a knock on the door and see a neighbor standing there with an empty bowl or other container of sorts looking to borrow a cup of flour or sugar. In the summertime, the neighborhood kids would often congregate on neighbors' lawns for games of kickball, wiffle ball, baseball, basketball, and countless other activities and competitions that kept us outside and away from our televisions and Atari 2600s.

We'd run around barefoot and have squirt gun fights as we jumped through water sprinklers and into each other's swimming pools. Sometimes we'd just get all of our *Star Wars* toys together and have one big galactic battle. At night we'd dress in dark clothes and play hide-and-seek with flashlights we'd pretend were lightsabers. We'd ride our bikes for hours on end and frequently venture off into the woods around our houses to explore, build forts, or play around a nearby manmade pond named "Haverty's Pond," in reference to the man whose property it was located on. At the top of the street was a vast blueberry field where we'd harvest the sweet berries in the summer and bring them home in large containers for our mothers to bake into muffins, pies, and pancakes. In the winter we'd build snow forts and have intense snowball fights. There were lots of trails and hills where we could go sledding, and when Haverty's Pond froze over we'd use it for ice-skating and hockey games. In short, there were countless things to do that kept us kids active and entertained throughout the year. It wasn't like today, when our children are glued to violent video games, their laptops, smartphones, tablets, and an endless variety of social media where one can claim to have hundreds of friends and not interact with a single one of them.

Things were certainly different then. As with the lifestyles of kids, the lifestyles of dogs were much different in those days in many respects as well—a point I will undoubtedly revisit again and again throughout this narrative. We live in a world today where animal owners tend to "humanize" their pets. In short, their pets are treated as equals to humans and afforded the same or nearly the same luxuries as their human possessors. Over the years this trend has been richly capitalized on by various industries that cater to animals. Today there are seemingly endless varieties of specialized and very costly high-end pet foods that are tailor-made for every type of animal and appropriate for whatever allergy or food intolerance the animal has—real or imaginary. Nowadays pets wear clothing and fashionable accessories such as jewelry and have access to virtually every kind of amusing toy the human mind can conceive. We spoil our animals in so many countless ways that it would be an exercise in sheer futility to try and list them all here. So why do I bother to bring the subject up? The answer is simple. As I chronicle Mandy's life and share with you some of the amusing and or sometimes sad parts of it, it's important for you to understand that what was considered "normal" dog care in the seventies and eighties could be seen as irresponsible or in some cases marginally cruel by today's standards. We shall delve into it a bit deeper now as I journey into the past and recall the life of my first dog.

The first problem my parents encountered with Mandy was her inability to be housebroken at the appropriate age. She quite frequently relieved herself whenever and wherever she saw fit while inside the house. Many a time as a youngster I remember stepping barefoot into a soggy and smelly part of the carpet where Mandy had done her business then retreated to another part of the house. Gradually the number of old newspapers began to multiply and blanket the areas where Mandy was known to squat frequently. They were of little help, however, as Mandy chose to ignore them and continue to "go" wherever she wanted. This would send my mother into a rage, and I can remember her angrily discussing the problem with my father on many occasions. Still being a "cat" person in those early months of having Mandy, my mother wouldn't hesitate to remind my father that cats were much cleaner and smarter than dogs and much more easily housebroken. It got to the point where our veterinarian warned my parents that if Mandy wasn't housebroken soon, she never would be. The problem persisted until Mandy had grown out of puppyhood. By some sheer miracle, my parents were finally able to housebreak her before it was too late. She held herself one night without having an accident until morning, when she was tied up in the backyard and free to "go" at her discretion.

Regrettably, Mandy spent the majority of her life tied up. It was common in those times to keep your dog leashed in the yard throughout the day, and many people did just that. Our house had a back deck with a long set of steps that led down into the backyard. My father had secured a suitable doghouse from our neighbors across the street and set it up for Mandy to use. (I remember we used my old metal wagon to transport it.) The doghouse was red with white trim and constructed of wood. It had a pitched roof with black tarpaper shingles. After placing it in the desired location, my father then strung a durable cable from a nearby tree and connected it to the side of the house several feet off the ground. At the center of this line he connected yet another line, which was firmly secured with hardware and would then attach to Mandy's collar.

Sadly, Mandy had a choke collar. Again, it was common for big dogs to have choke collars in those days, as they were used to restrain the dog from excessive pulling on their leash and as a corrective tool when training. I know that if I could jump in Doc Brown's DeLorean and rev it up to 88mph and travel back to the early eighties, one of the first things I'd do would be replace that choke collar with a more conventional one. Regrettably though, I can't change the past, and Mandy had to live with that choke collar her entire life.

Mandy's outside living area was carved out of a portion of our backyard. The doghouse was at the center. From there, Mandy had a circumference of about thirty feet, in which she could roam in most directions. She did not like being chained and would often pace back and forth endlessly at the outermost fringe of her boundary. Over time, she wore a semi-circular path right into the earth, where nothing but dirt remained and not a single blade of grass could grow. Her outside living space was an area I referred to as her "pen." I'm not sure if it was necessarily the correct or appropriate term to use, but it stuck, and everybody in the neighborhood started calling it "Mandy's Pen." On days it rained, the bare earth exposed from the constant pacing she did would turn into a morass of mud that would coat her paws and legs in a thick brown slop. The mud would dry and cake onto her scraggly, long-coated underside creating an unholy mess of dried dirt that couldn't be brushed out but only washed off. If left unattended, Mandy would deposit small mounds of dirt throughout the house whenever she lay down. This of course infuriated my mother, who ultimately was responsible for cleaning up the mess (and the dog, for that matter).

My mother deserves the most credit when discussing the overall care of not only Mandy, but also every pet my parents have owned for the past forty-plus years. For it was my mother who reliably and unfailingly fed, bathed, brushed, clipped, exercised, and doctored all our animals. My brother and I had everyday duties concerning Mandy, but we were both young, lazy, and inattentive to her everyday needs. One of my jobs was to put her out in the morning and bring her in at night. I would do so, but usually had to be constantly reminded by my mother. I also was tasked with feeding her. Mandy was fed once a day at night just after she was let in. The task required me to simply open a can of Skippy dog food and mix it with some dry Come 'N Get It. It was hardly difficult, but as a young boy it was something I didn't want to be bothered with, as it ultimately pulled me away from my toys or the television. Nevertheless, I did do it when told, but ultimately the responsibility was routinely thrust on my mother, who was busy enough trying to run a household with as little chaos as possible—not an easy task in those days or even now.

My mother was a homemaker, as were the majority of women in those days. She had a degree in French, and for a brief time held a teaching job that supported both her and my father shortly after they were married.

When my brother was born in 1971, as my father was starting out into what would become a long career in the truck leasing business, my mother became a dedicated housewife. I was born in 1973, and my mother certainly had her hands full at that time. She wanted kids and to be a mother. She believed that it was a mother's responsibility to raise decent children and not a nanny, babysitter, or daycare provider. Looking back, and judging by today's standards, my mother sacrificed a lot (if not all) of her time for her family. She took care of my brother and me during the day while my father was at work. She drove us to every birthday party, sports practice, doctor's appointment, or any other important or trivial event in our lives. She attended every parent–teacher conference and volunteered for various school-related events, such as field trips and sports team booster clubs. She was always home for us and very involved in every aspect of our young lives. She definitely was in charge of the day-to-day operations of the Morin household, as she cooked, cleaned, and managed the care, of my brother, Mandy, and me—every day.

My father deserves equal credit, but in a different manner. Like most husbands of the time, he went off to work every morning. In my opinion, he believed his primary responsibility was to provide for his family through gainful employment. He made sure his family always had a solid roof over their heads, food on the table, decent clothes on their backs, and presents under the Christmas tree. He taught my brother and I responsibility and how to work hard to accomplish our goals. He rewarded us whenever we showed initiative to mow the lawn, clip the hedges, stack firewood, shovel snow out of the driveway, or help fix something around the house. He taught us right from wrong and didn't tolerate bad or disrespectful behavior from us toward others. He often would come home from work in the evening and give my mother a well-deserved rest by playing with my brother and me and occupying us long enough for her to regain some of her strength—and possibly sanity.

My father's job often had him traveling out of state to help grow his company's business. Oftentimes he was away for a few days a week. In recent years he has expressed regret over those early times of frequent travel and wondered if they were detrimental to the family. I have told him on more than one occasion that at no time growing up did I ever feel neglected or overlooked during his absences. My mother would take my brother and me to the airport to greet my father as he got off the plane—during the days when you actually *could* greet someone getting directly off the plane—after long business trips. I enjoyed those times because I was always happy to see my father come home. As a youth, and even today, I've always said that if I could be just like my father, I'd be a very happy person. I couldn't ask for a better role model.

If the Morin household was viewed as a company, my father was the CEO and my mother was the Vice President of Operations. My brother, Mandy, and I were the employees, guided by my father, and under close supervision and direction from my mother. Though two young boys are a handful under any circumstances, it was Mandy that would prove to be the biggest challenge to my parents and to the family overall. Her behavior, personality, and penchant for causing mischief would test all those who knew her.

Mandy, for lack of a kinder way of putting it, was extremely dumb. "Numb" is how my father frequently referred to her. Perhaps it was the times, the sheer lack of canine obedience schools, or simply my young family's inexperience with dogs that fueled Mandy's lack of natural intelligence, but, try as we might, none of us could get her to mind on command.

I tried the hardest. As a young boy, I was fascinated with the thought of getting her to obey me and do tricks. I would shout out commands while waving tempting Milk-Bone treats in her face. This usually resulted in her simply overpowering me, snatching the Milk-Bone from my fingers and not obeying a single thing I said. We tried to train her for what seemed like an eternity, but nothing ever stuck. Over time she recognized her name when spoken, but did not ever take it to mean "come here" as it was intended to do. Sometimes she would come—usually with the help of a treat in hand—but more often than not she would just ignore you. And if she were loose in the neighborhood, and you called her name to get her to stop and come back to the house, forget about it. That *never* worked.

Over the course of her life, Mandy only acknowledged three distinct voice commands. She acknowledged her name, she acknowledged "sit" and she acknowledged "lie down." I say "acknowledged" because she understood she was supposed to do something when one of those three commands was spoken. However, she never fully understood what each command meant. To illustrate, I would often tell her to lie down, whereupon she would promptly sit. I would then get her on her feet again and say, "Sit," whereupon she would lie down on the floor. My favorite was to hold up a Milk-Bone and watch her sit, then lie down, then get back up again, then lie down, then whimper, then twirl around in a circle before I even had a chance to utter a command! I always made sure to reward her with a treat when she obeyed correctly, but those times were so few and far between, that it didn't even seem worth the effort. Mandy would spend her life untrained.

Unfortunately, Mandy's lack of obedience, I suspect, fueled her desire to openly rebel. As I mentioned earlier, she was leashed outside during the day when the weather was agreeable. (She was not kept outside if it was raining or snowing hard or if the temperature was excessively hot or cold.) She had an untamable desire to slip her collar and run wild. Freedom was foremost on her mind, and rightfully so. She was leashed her whole life. She had no desire to run away from her family permanently—we loved her and she loved us—but she took advantage of every opportunity to run hard and run free whenever she could get away. Occasionally she found a way to wiggle out of her collar, and when she did she took off like a rocket. Fortunately we lived on a quiet dead-end street with little traffic and lots of surrounding woods. She never headed for the main road of Washington Avenue, but was more enticed by the woods and Haverty's Pond behind our house. She was never gone for very long and occasionally would wander back to our house on her own, but that was extremely rare. Usually a neighbor or one of the neighborhood kids who was able to grasp her collar and lead her home would bring her back to us. You can imagine how difficult this task was at night since she was a black dog and hard enough to find in the woods during the day. Without fail, however, we always found her and got her home safe. She was always soaked and covered in mud, but never harmed. My biggest dread was that she would be killed by running out in front of a fast-moving car.

Mandy's wild side wasn't suppressed when she was in the safe confines of the house either. You always had to keep one eye on her, because she chewed virtually everything she could easily get her jaws around. She chewed furniture, pillows, shoes, sports equipment, and most anything she could pick out of the trash. But most disturbing to me was her ruthless and relentless assault on my toys, particularly my prized *Star Wars* toys and action figures. Any tantalizing toy left out that was in her grasp was most assuredly damaged, destroyed, or, in rare cases, totally ingested! I can't even begin to describe the number of small toy accessories and *Lego* blocks that dog consumed. And that was just what I witnessed. I can't imagine what went down her gullet when I wasn't looking. I had one of the largest *Star Wars* toy collections in the neighborhood. Toys that I treasured but didn't necessarily take good care of. All I can say is that if Mandy hadn't declared her own personal war on *both* the Rebel Alliance and the Empire, I'd have a lot more vintage *Star Wars* toys in my collection today and quite possibly more money in my bank account!

I wasn't the only victim of Mandy's relentless chewing habit, however. My brother's baseball gloves were often favorite targets of hers. And most curiously, my father's tools were often attacked. My father is quite handy and was often fixing things around the house. He had two hammers that had black rubber-coated handles that enticed Mandy to no end. She got ahold of one of them and went to town on it. She almost completely chewed the end off, leaving nothing but the exposed metal base showing. The second hammer was attacked too but survived with much less damage. I am proud to say that both those hammers remain in my father's workshop to this day. They are still used and kept as mementoes of Mandy's memory. She even chewed a select number of shingles on the side of the house! We gave her chew toys and tennis balls in hopes that it would spare some of our meager possessions from annihilation, but ultimately they didn't satiate her enough, and she kept chewing until she eventually and curiously grew out of it.

Another troubling trait of Mandy's was her inability to be left alone. There were times in the evening when the family would go out to dinner, a banquet, a school award ceremony, a sporting event, or some other social function that would require Mandy to be left alone in the house for a few hours. Upon return, we would often find the house trashed, and Mandy would be cowering in her little den behind my father's recliner in the living room. The trash bucket in the kitchen was her first target. She'd knock it over, eat anything she considered edible, and proceed to scatter the rest throughout the house. She'd pull the pillows off the furniture and sometimes shred them. She'd chew the legs of the furniture. She'd knock over stools and kitchen table chairs, and proceed to chew up any toys, magazines, newspapers or other things of that nature within her reach. Astonishingly, she often got at items on the countertop as well as on top of the refrigerator! Oftentimes the house looked like it had been burglarized. Once the shock of what had happened had passed, my parents would harshly scold the dog and spank her to hopefully convey the message that what she had done was bad.

It never worked though. She continued to trash the house whenever we left her alone. We would lock up the garbage in a closet, put things away and out of reach, close bedroom doors, and make sure she was well-fed before leaving. This only minimized the damage she would do and actually exacerbated the problem. In my opinion, by restricting her access to only two or three rooms of the house, we encouraged her to rebel even more and be more destructive. We didn't necessarily realize it at the time, but it was obvious that Mandy suffered from some form of separation anxiety. As she got older, the problem lessened until she was eventually free of it and could be trusted to be left alone. I should also mention that we did whatever we could to prevent situations where she was forced to be by herself. However, it was difficult in those days, as animals were not as freely accepted in places like they are today, and it wasn't necessarily in pet owners minds to take their animals everywhere like many do today. The saddest thing I ever had to watch my father do with Mandy was put her in a kennel when the family went on vacation. She would look so sad and tremble when we checked her in. I couldn't wait to go get her when we got home. She'd ride in my lap in the car with her head stuck out the passenger side window happy as a clam.

One small but interesting event that showcases Mandy's destructive nature was a time when my mother fried up some hamburgers for dinner and allowed my brother and me to eat them in the living room as we watched television—a rare treat in those days. She put the plates down on the hassock, which we proceeded to use as a little table. Mandy immediately zeroed in on the hot food that was conveniently right at her level. She wasted no time and directly went for our dishes. We pushed her away, commanded her to "get lost," and did everything else possible to prevent her from overpowering us and devouring our dinner. We were rapidly losing the battle, however. Finally I got up and grabbed Mandy by the collar and pulled her into my bedroom. I closed the door behind me thinking that I had solved our problem and could now eat my meal in peace while watching TV. Well, I had solved one problem but immediately created a far worse one—at least in my parents' eyes. While my brother and I happily ate our burgers, an unsettling scratching sound began to emanate from the bedroom. The sound intensified until we got up to investigate. Upon opening the door to my room, Mandy shot out and immediately raced downstairs. I remember looking down and seeing the corner of my bedroom carpet at the base of the door all torn up. Mandy, not wanting to be confined, immediately decided to try and dig her way out! As if on cue, she realized what she had done was wrong, and immediately went to seek refuge downstairs until my father cooled off. Needless to say, both my parents were infuriated, not only at the dog but at me!

I have one more story that I consider the grand finale, personifying Mandy's rebellious and destructive nature. I'm reminded of it every year on Halloween. One cool autumn night in late October, when I was seven or eight years old, my father was away on business and my mother found herself needing something from the drug store. Not wanting to leave my brother and me home alone at night, even briefly, she put us in the car and we sped off in search of whatever it was she required. Mandy was left behind inside the house. When we returned shortly thereafter, I remember my mother inserting the house key into the lock of the front door and then trying to push it open…without success. The door was jammed shut and we couldn't figure out why. Fortunately, there was a long, vertical window that was next to our front door. There was just enough light inside the house to see that there was a broomstick jammed between the inside of the front door and one of the brown carpeted stairs that led up into the house. It looked as if someone had deliberately barricaded the front door from the inside.

I don't know what was going through my mother's head at that exact moment, but I'm sure she was nervous and had thoughts of potentially running into a burglar. Nevertheless, she persevered and managed to get the door open just enough so that either my brother or I could slip our skinny arms in and dislodge the broomstick. The second the door swung open and my mother stepped inside, Mandy came slowly slinking down the stairs and slipped out the front door with her head down. Either my brother or I grabbed her before she could take off, and it immediately became apparent to us that she knew she had been bad and wanted to go hide in shame.

What we saw when we entered the house and got all the lights on was beyond belief. Mandy had had a major meltdown and destroyed or damaged just about everything she could get into. The trash was strewn throughout the house; pillows, couch cushions and bedspreads had been chewed up, magazines shredded and furniture clawed. Family pictures were knocked over and several of my toys were destroyed. It was clearly one of the worst incidents we had ever experienced with our dog. But despite all she had done and destroyed, there was one thing that stood out above all else. At the time it was very close to Halloween and my mother had purchased a large red and white bag of Nestle $100,000 candy bars—now known as 100 Grand bars. She was planning to pass them out to trick-or-treaters and had them stored on top of the refrigerator. Among all the debris strewn across the kitchen floor was the large red and white plastic bag—empty! We found some candy wrappers here and there, but we quickly determined that Mandy had eaten the contents of the entire candy bag. The fact that she had ingested what would easily be considered a lethal dose of chocolate for dogs was startling enough, but what was even more amazing was that she had clearly devoured most of the wrappers along with the candy! It was not widely known that chocolate was bad, and possibly lethal, for dogs to ingest in those days, and we thought that she would simply be sick to her stomach and, at worst, just puke. To my knowledge, she never got sick from the chocolate, and she certainly didn't die.

When the dust settled we were more than astonished at what she had done. To commit the amount of damage she had and to get at all the things she had sunk her teeth into required her to leap up on the kitchen counters, the living room furniture, and possibly the kitchen table itself. To picture her standing on the countertops was inconceivable. I wondered if this was yet another act of rebellion, as Mandy was never allowed on the furniture and would be yelled at if she tried to climb up on a chair, a bed, or the couch. And how did she ever get the broomstick so perfectly wedged between the door and the stairs? It felt like she knew exactly what she was doing and tried to keep us out as long as possible. I'm still bewildered by it all today.

After that night I was afraid my parents would take drastic action against the dog. There were times I wondered if Mandy would be sent to a pound or some animal shelter because she was so incorrigible. How much could my parents take? Our dog was literally destroying our home. I'm sure they discussed their options in detail and in a sense I'm glad I never heard their conversations. Despite all her problems, I loved Mandy very much and wanted her to stay. In the end, my parents decided that ridding the family of Mandy would be too traumatic for my brother and me. The dog would stay, and we'd deal with the consequences whatever they'd be. I think it's interesting to mention that to this day, the Nestle 100 Grand bar is one of my favorite candy bars. It was when I was a kid, and it still is now. I buy a bag of the luscious red-wrapped bars every October. And the ones I don't manage to eat I pass out to my neighborhood's trick-or-treaters. I do this faithfully every year in remembrance of Mandy and the remarkable destruction she wrought that night so many years ago.

Unfortunately, to this point I've cast a mostly disparaging light on Mandy. I've focused a lot on some of the more troubling stories involving her oftentimes naughty and reckless nature. And though there are other reproachful tales I could impart (and will undoubtedly touch on later in this narrative), it's important for me to stress that Mandy had many positive qualities as well—at least in the eyes of a young boy. Thinking back to those days, a smile creeps across my face when remembering some of the helpful, mischievous, and even lovable qualities she possessed.

Mandy was a barker. She barked at anyone and everything for virtually any reason. She'd bark at any stranger (man or beast) that unknowingly breached her territory or even someone she knew and trusted just dropping by for a visit. Usually the barking was short-lived and generally she'd stop after being scolded by a family member. There wasn't a delivery person who visited our house in those years who hadn't heard the ferocious bark of Mandy. Whether tied up out back or roaming freely inside the house, little slipped her attention. She came off as very tough and had quite the ferocious act once she got into character. Fortunately, it was just that—an act. I do know for a fact that her loud barking and aggressive posturing put genuine fear in the hearts of many who witnessed it. I also know that virtually none of those people understood how big a coward she really was. Mandy was the personification of the phrase, "Her bark is worse than her bite." First let me state that she never bit or caused injury to anyone—ever. Second, if you truly challenged her one on one, you would have found out very quickly that she was mostly incapable of executing any kind of real threat. She'd bark, growl, snarl, and occasionally jump up on you (in a playful way), but every step you took toward her was met with two steps of retreat. In fact, her act was so funny to watch, I often goaded her into one of her ferocious postures so I could laugh at her fake bark and watch her pathetic retreat. Once someone realized that her performance was pure theater, they found that the barking would stop fairly quickly and that she was more apt to come up and lick your face rather than take a bite out of your leg.

Why do I consider Mandy's thespian exploits of ferocity positive? Well, for one, they were entertaining, and secondly they were useful. Fortunately I was not bullied much as a child, but I grew up on a street dominated mostly by boys of varying ages. Fights happened, and kids were teased and picked on. I was not immune to either. There were plenty of times I felt threatened and outnumbered. Not wanting to fight unless I absolutely had to, I often ran to the safety of Mandy's pen. I knew that if I could make it into her range, I would be safe. The second any kid tried to pursue me into her sphere of influence, she'd leap up and go into her ferocious little act. It was such a relief to see any bully stop dead in his tracks the second I crossed the threshold into Mandy's little world. She was my unofficial bodyguard, and I made sure to reward her with a treat the first chance I got—generally when my mother wasn't looking.

Mandy helped me out of many jams as a kid. Since she was so destructive in her early years, it was easy to blame her whenever something of value got lost or broken. I hate to admit it now, but I framed her for many crimes she didn't actually commit. However, my parents were smarter than I thought in those days and more often than not I was inevitably found guilty. However, once in a while I'd slip one by them and Mandy would have to take the fall. But it was all good since Mandy couldn't really be punished. She might get scolded or tied up in the yard a little longer than normal, but it was nothing compared to the punishment I would have incurred. In my young mind, it was a win-win situation.

As a young child, one of my all-time favorite qualities of Mandy's was her seemingly unstoppable ability to ingest any type of food in any quantity. As I've mentioned earlier, she would eat just about anything. Mandy loved to beg at the dinner table and she got her fair share of table scraps even though it was a rule not to feed her. Once Mandy had scarfed down her own food, she would quickly scurry over to the table to see what else could be had. She had a kind of passive-aggressive approach to her begging. When she was feeling saucy, she'd gently pant, whine, and rock back and forth in hopes some food would be graciously and willingly tossed in her direction. More times than not, this approach failed miserably and one or both of my parents ordered her away from the table. In time she developed a more subtle approach and would stealthily encamp under the table. There she would quietly lay in wait hoping for spilled food to tumble down her way. (Peas were always at the top of the list.)

Occasionally, my mother would prepare a meal that I just wasn't crazy about. To this day I've never seen my father not thoroughly clean his plate. He'd scrape it down with his fork until every morsel of food and blot of sauce was completely gone. My brother had a voracious appetite too and ate just about everything put in front of him in amounts and at speeds that would astonish most. I on the other hand was pickier and not as thorough with consuming my meal. The problem grew exponentially when I was served a dish I didn't like, which happens with every kid growing up. My mother occasionally fixed a dish called "Hamburger Pie." My father loved it and encouraged her to make it often. My brother wolfed it down without issue either. I, however, couldn't stand it. Then and even today, it's a meal I can't stomach. The recipe was rather simple. My mother would take ground hamburger and press it into a pie plate. When she was done, the meat resembled a piecrust. She'd then add stewed tomatoes, (possibly some other ingredients I'm not readily recalling), and cover the whole mess, (yes, I said *mess*), with cheese. In to the oven it would go and come out looking like a big cheesy pie. I didn't like the way it looked, I hated the way it smelled, and I couldn't stand the way it tasted. Somehow the combination of the melted cheese, stewed tomatoes, and ground beef didn't light my fire in any way, and I secretly felt like crying every time a slice of that gooey mess, (yes, I said *mess* again), was placed in front of me.

Without fail, I was always the last one seated at the table when Hamburger Pie was served. My father, having finished his meal, would retreat to the living room to watch the evening news, while my brother would go off and find something to do that would amuse him. I was left at the table alone pondering what to do. My mother would linger in the kitchen and scold me for not eating my meal. She tried most anything, but nothing encouraged me to want to take a bite. As a last resort she'd cut up the pie slice into small pieces, often separating out the hamburger that she knew I liked. She'd then offer me liberal amounts of ketchup for dipping, as she knew that would help. Sometimes that would work and I would eat the meat, but I could never willingly bring myself to eat any of the stewed tomatoes now suffocating under a coagulated mess of cold cheese. What to do?

Eventually my mother would get frustrated and become very angry with me. As a last resort, she'd point to some uneaten portion on my plate and order me to eat just that part. If I could do that, then I could be excused. I would agree and wait for the opportunity to put my master plan in motion. All I needed was for something to happen that would draw my mother away from the table and out of the kitchen. She might need to run to the bathroom, or better yet the phone would ring, forcing her to get up and answer it while keeping her distracted as she talked. No matter what it was, the second she was out of sight, I uncorked my secret weapon.

Mandy would always loiter silently under the table. At times she was stealthy enough where she was totally forgotten about. She always camped close to my feet since she knew there was a better chance of getting food from me than from either my brother or my father. To put it simply, over the years I must have gorged that dog on Hamburger Pie and every other food I didn't like to eat. Mandy saved me so many times that I can't begin to recollect them all. I was meticulous and patiently waited for my moment. When it arrived, I stuffed the unwanted food down her bottomless gullet, and she was only too happy to receive it. We were like a team working together. Over the years, sneaking Mandy food became somewhat of an art of mine. Mandy played her part well also. She ate quickly and developed this subtle and innocent look whenever challenged. It was interesting to see and I can still recall how she looked then.

Despite our efforts, more often than not I was caught and severely disciplined verbally and sometimes physically, but every once in a while I'd (I should say "we'd") pull it off without a hitch. For some reason it was always worth the risk. Mandy was never punished, as she was seen only as a "witless accessory" to the crime. I on the other hand received the full brunt of my mother's justice. But like I said, it was always worth the risk. Mandy had my back whenever it came to quick food disposal. I could always count on her for that.

Mandy provided good companionship too. She loved to be petted and have her belly scratched. Oftentimes in the winter evenings she and I would disappear down into the family room where she'd curl up in front of the warm wood stove and I'd lounge on the couch and watch PBS, (no cable on our family room TV), or play Atari games. She was always good company when she wasn't in the house alone. Occasionally I'd let her sneak up onto the couch with me. She was naughty a lot, but she was always my friend.

Though I often feel sad knowing that Mandy spent the majority of her life leashed, there was one point in her young life where she experienced what could only be described as pure heaven to her. In 1979, my parents were toying with the notion of moving from Portland to Falmouth, an adjacent town. My father purchased a piece of undeveloped land in Falmouth with the intention of clearing a lot and building a new house. The area was much more rural, private, and secluded than the neighborhood street we lived on in Portland. The privacy appealed to my father as well as the idea of building a new house. The property was located at the top of a long dirt road just off the main street called Middle Road. It was set back deep into the woods. My father started to bring my brother, Mandy and me to what he called "The Lot" on weekends. Once there, armed with a chainsaw, gas and oil, various handsaws, a splitting maul, tools of all sorts, toilet paper (for emergencies), a BB gun or two, and a trailer for hauling wood, my father proceeded to fell and cut up trees, thus carving out space for what would become our new house lot.

At the time, I was too young to be of any real help to my father. His goal, as far as I was concerned, was to keep me busy with menial tasks—more importantly, out of danger. I spent a lot of time lugging brush out of the way and stacking piles of freshly split wood onto the trailer. My brother, on the other hand, was just old enough to contribute more meaningfully. He was allowed to use the axe and some of the bigger handsaws to help clear out smaller trees and split wood. He was even allowed to drive a tractor my father used up there in later years to haul away large logs. I desperately wanted to drive the tractor, but my father refused, saying that I was still too young.

As far as Mandy was concerned, I saw my father do something with her that I had never seen before in my life. He let her out of the family's green and white Chevy van, removed her choke collar and let her take off at full speed into the woods without saying a word. I was horrified the first time I saw him do this. Up until then, all I had ever known was that Mandy being loose was a bad thing. I nearly chased after her.

"Let her go. She'll be all right. She's not going to run off," said my father.

I didn't know it then, but my father had just granted our dog her first taste of real freedom. His plan was to let her run free all day while we worked. There was plenty of woods for her to explore and virtually no danger of her running onto Middle Road and getting hit by a car. After the initial shock of what he had done wore off, my mind quickly focused on other things, and I can honestly say that my worries gradually evaporated. We would work throughout the day. At times, I remember hearing Mandy crash through the woods in the distance, and occasionally I'd see her racing along the tree line, but overall, hours would pass and I had no idea where she was. My father claims to this day that he always knew her whereabouts and that she never wandered very far off. This may be true, but I find it hard to believe, even now. There had to have been times when even he didn't know where she was. Though I never saw it, my father has also stated in the past that on particularly hot days Mandy would often run herself to exhaustion, come back and slurp down a gallon of water we provided for her, then go off and curl up under a shady tree and happily go to sleep. One thing I do remember vividly was Mandy always showing up at noontime once lunch was brought out. Occasionally my mother would make a surprise visit and provide us with a treat from Burger King. The second the scent of hot food filled the air, you'd hear that familiar crashing through the brush followed by the appearance of an always wet and usually muddy Mandy.

The days at "The Lot" were sometimes fun times despite all the work we did. I liked being outside and playing in the woods. It was a very quiet and peaceful place when the sound of my father's chainsaw didn't fill the air. Sometimes we'd go up there just for fun. We'd shoot BB guns at paper targets and go exploring in the woods. Rest assured, Mandy was with us on every trip. When the workday was over, my father would load up the van and we'd be off to get our reward for the day, which amounted to a frosty treat from Dairy Queen. My brother and I were just young and dumb enough to think that a Dilly Bar and a hot fudge sundae were the perfect forms of payment for a day's work cutting and stacking wood. Believe me, my father took full advantage; he knew that the days where we'd be hounding him for cash as payment for work done around the house, or in general, were not far off. Mandy on the other hand could not be happier with her "doggie dish" of vanilla that she devoured in record time. What more could she ask for? What better existence was there on earth than a day of untethered freedom romping through the woods of Falmouth? And what more could our dog want than to have her play day topped off with an ice cream? I can only imagine that this period in her life was the happiest experience she had ever known in her entire existence.

I can remember riding home from "The Lot" one evening. It was a warm summer night and the sun was setting. The windows were down and a steady stream of inviting, warm air flowed over my face. The van was very quiet as my father drove in silence, his arm out the window and my brother lazily snoozing in the front seat. I looked in the back and was surprised not to see Mandy. Normally she was very active whenever in the car. She would fidget, whine, and bark at things while constantly moving from window to window. She was also always one to want to be up front so she could stick her head out the passenger side window. However, this time she was curiously quiet and absent from her normal riding routine. I remember looking under the van's back seat. All curled up in a ball and fast asleep was Mandy, her Dairy Queen doggie dish lying haphazardly nearby and licked clean. To this day I can still see her face. Her eyes were closed and it looked as if she was smiling as she slept. I had never seen her so content in my whole life. I almost wished the ride home were lengthier so that my dog could have her slice of heaven for just a bit longer.

Sadly, the house in Falmouth never materialized despite all the clearing we did. My parents came to the decision to remain in Portland and my father ended up selling "The Lot" in 1984. Just like that, after just a few short years, Mandy's paradise was gone. I have often wondered what it would have been like if we had moved to Falmouth and built a house on that lot. Would Mandy have been tied up like before, or would she have been allowed to roam freely? Unfortunately we'll never know. I'm just glad she had the time that she did up there. I can say quite confidently that it was most assuredly her favorite place. Today, instead of a solitary dirt road that cuts into the woods off Middle Road, there are multiple paved roads that lead up to several privately owned houses close to where our old lot used to be. It's still a fairly rural area, but much more developed now than it was in the early eighties. Nowadays I drive by it from time to time. Each time I do, I'm reminded of Mandy and her little slice of paradise.

I think it's important to mention one other place where Mandy got to experience the world outside her pen at home. My father liked to fish and wasted no time introducing the pastime to my brother and me when we were old enough. For many years, my father co-owned a series of boats that he purchased jointly with a friend of his. They were primarily meant for lake fishing and ranged on average from eighteen to twenty-two feet in length. Since we lived so close to the ocean, and since my father had done some recreational lobstering, occasionally we'd venture out into the relative safety of Casco Bay to do some fishing or pleasure boating. One hot summer day in July of 1985, my father took me out for a day of boating on the ocean. Mandy, of course, came with us. I don't believe she had ever been on a boat before and surely had no knowledge of the ocean. Nevertheless she was excited as always. Off went the choke collar and into the boat went Mandy. We cruised around Casco Bay. I sat up in the bow and watched Mandy rush from one side of the vessel to the other trying to take everything in.

After cruising around the bay and doing some light fishing, we navigated to Sand Island, a small, uninhabited 1.5-acre island off Great Chebeague. We anchored the boat and made our way ashore. We had the entire island to ourselves, and Mandy couldn't be happier. She ran along the sandy beach and up and down the rocks. She jumped into the ocean and ran up on shore to roll around in the sand. It was like being at "The Lot" again. Mandy had found a new paradise.

We ate lunch and lounged on the beach. I set a crab trap in the shallows and tried to catch small crabs or anything foolish enough to venture into my underwater snare. Mandy and I fooled around in the sand, played fetch, and explored the cool surroundings. Overall it was a great day. We all had lots of fun. When it started to get late, we returned to the boat to do some last minute cruising before heading back to port. I remember the water got a little choppy and the boat tossed a bit. Unfortunately, Mandy, having no knowledge or experience with the ocean and not knowing the difference between fresh water and seawater, began to get thirsty and lap up small pools of the salty brine that splashed into the boat. It wasn't long before we noticed her mood change. Instead of rushing around the boat in her normal hyper manner, she suddenly became very lethargic and spread out flat on the deck. It became readily apparent that she was seasick and dehydrated after ingesting seawater. Before we could react, she puked all over the deck. We rushed her a bowl of fresh water that she slurped down instantly. Once we got out of the chop and into calmer waters and after we got her rehydrated, she made a fast recovery and bounced back to her old self. She learned a valuable lesson that day. Don't drink seawater. My father hoped she got the message, as I'm sure he was very unhappy. For he was the one who had to clean up the puke! The day was such a success that we returned to Sand Island in the summer of 1987, not only with the dog, but also with my older brother and my paternal grandmother. I know Mandy was thrilled to see her oceanic paradise one more time. I always think of it as her island nowadays.

As the early eighties gave way to the mid eighties, my family did eventually move. In October of 1985, we ventured off Lester Drive and moved into a much larger house located less than a mile away from our old home! In was situated on busy Auburn Street and is still the current residence of my parents today. The new house (new to us, that is, as it was built back in the fifties) was considerably larger than our old homestead, with many interesting perks that captivated both my brother and me. He was fourteen and I was eleven when we moved in. The first noticeable difference was the size. It was much more spacious than our previous home. It had multiple rooms spanning three levels. My brother saw the house before me and conveniently claimed his bedroom before I even had a chance to challenge him for it. The sole reason he picked the room was because it had a built in air conditioner— a luxury unheard of at the time for a fourteen-year-old's room. I managed to score big too, though I didn't really appreciate it back then. My bedroom was the largest in the house. Ironically, my parents' bedroom was the smallest. In total, the house had four bedrooms, two full bathrooms, a half-bath, a large living room, a decent kitchen area, a "sunken" living room where the main TV was placed, a smaller TV room, and an enormous basement that contained my father's workshop, office, and additional storage rooms. Our new home also had a small game room where a pool table was kept.

All these new amenities, fascinating and fresh as they were, paled in comparison to what lay outside in the backyard. Behind the house was a heated, in-ground swimming pool. Beside the fact that we had never had a pool, the most interesting and novel characteristic about this particular one was that it was under an inflatable dome. The simple flip of a switch inside the house activated a blower that pumped in air and inflated it. Deflated, the dome looked and acted like an ingenuous pool cover. But when the blower underneath was engaged, it slowly came to life and rose up to form a bubble-shaped shelter that allowed us to swim safely in bad weather, at night, and free of insects. It was truly remarkable and my favorite thing about the new house. Additionally, adjacent to the pool was a concrete deck and a nice cabana where we could conveniently change clothes and store pool toys. There was also a nice stone barbeque fireplace that was rarely used but pleasing to the eye. I remember enjoying several pool parties with lots of food, music, and fun in that spacious backyard.

The humans of the family weren't the only ones to benefit from the magnificent house upgrade. Mandy had it pretty good too. Her new "pen" in the backyard was significantly larger than her old one. Additionally, my father set her up with a "dog trolley" attached to a central line strung between two trees. This new apparatus allowed her to wander more freely and unhampered. Her old doghouse was put in the center of the run, and she had lots of shady trees to keep cool under during hot summer days. (I failed to mention earlier that this new house had lots of woods surrounding it on three sides and no neighboring houses lined up next to it like our old residence.) Also, keeping true to form, it wasn't long before Mandy's habitual pacing carved out a brand new path along the fringe of her pen.

Inside the house, Mandy had it pretty good too. She enjoyed the larger space and took full advantage of it. It wasn't long before she claimed her own little personal places that normally were located behind furniture or near windows. She adapted well to her new home and settled in quickly and easily. Unfortunately the same couldn't be said for our three cats. (It should be noted that after Sam my family had a varying number of cats from 1980 to 1998. Mandy was never without feline companionship throughout the course of her life. The Morin cats will only be mentioned briefly in this narrative as the focus here is on the dogs, but it is only fair to mention that our cats are worthy of their own book—which may come later.)

I think the move was good for Mandy. She was now a full-grown, adult dog and had seemingly matured out of her destructive phase. Oh, there were still minor incidents, but nothing that compared to her daring Lester Drive exploits. As she grew older she became more docile, but the fiery yearning to run free never abandoned her—even in her final months.

Mandy was not an ideal dog for walking. I tried to walk her many times over the course of her life with the results always being drearily the same. To put it simply, she pulled for all she was worth. She would test her choke collar to the very limits and pull just shy of strangling herself to death. As I've said before, she was not a very intelligent dog, but she knew just how far she could push the collar before injuring herself. That, I'm certain, she had down to a science. She would pull, and pull, and pull, until I thought my arm would be wrenched out of the socket. The only reprieve I'd get was when she stopped to sniff something or relieve herself. I honestly believe the walking leash confused Mandy. She understood being tied up in the confines of her pen, and she had experienced the unbridled freedom of running at the wood lot. But being walked in a park or simply down the street must have confused her. When walked, she was being introduced to new places, and I think she registered it as meaning an imminent opportunity to run free. However, she was constrained by a leash. The only real time she was leashed was when she was tied up for the day in her pen. So by that logic, I believe she didn't understand being walked. In her mind, I believe all she understood was either being tied up in a very familiar and confined area, or visiting a new area whereupon she would inevitably be let loose and be able to explore freely. I don't want to give the impression that she was never taken anywhere—she was—but she always was leashed as the risk of her bolting and getting hit by a car or some other form of heavy machinery was too great…which now leads me to a very memorable yet scary incident.

Mandy was a bit more clever than any of us truly gave her credit for. Several times over the course of her life on Lester Drive, Mandy had been able to slip her collar and dash off into the woods ringing the neighborhood. She was in little danger then, as the greatest threat, that of being hit by a car on Washington Avenue, was minimal. However, the danger was magnified exponentially once we moved to Auburn Street. The house faced the very heavily traveled road where traffic fresh off the turnpike would scream by almost non-stop during the day. It didn't help matters that our house sat astride a long and straight stretch of road where it was easy for a car to get up to speed very quickly. The danger of Mandy getting loose and into the road always lingered on my mind in those days.

One winter evening, I was instructed to go get Mandy and let her in the house for the night. As I had done hundreds of times before in my life, I wandered out back and unhooked her from her trolley. Normally, the sight of someone coming to get and bring her in the house put Mandy into a state of excitement. She'd leap up or pace wildly back and forth until directly confronted. At that point someone, (usually me), would insert his or her middle finger (because it was the largest and strongest finger, not because we wanted to flip our dog the bird) through the looped end of her choke collar, which would pull it tight around her neck and keep her restrained while we walked her in. This was normally how it was done. Over the years, particularly when she got older and more subdued, I (and other family members) got into the habit of occasionally unhooking her and allowing her to trot freely up to the house where she would briefly wait to be let inside. We got all too comfortable with this, and that night I really got burned.

It was chilly out and Mandy stood there looking pathetic. Her head hung limply and there wasn't any indication that she wanted to do anything but slowly shuffle inside the house, devour her food, then find a quiet and warm place to lie down. Little did I know what was about to happen the second I unhooked her. As the trolley hook dropped to the ground, Mandy stepped forward slowly and cautiously. She picked her head up and looked back at me. I swear the second she realized that I wasn't going to take her by the collar and escort her inside, she sprang to life and took off! I had unknowingly taken the bait. She had duped me into thinking she would quietly walk up to the back steps and into the house. I couldn't have been more wrong.

To my absolute horror, Mandy didn't head into the back woods as she had done so many times before when she had gotten loose. Instead, she ran full throttle up the paved road that wrapped around the side of the house and into the driveway. From there, her afterburners kicked in, and without a split second of hesitation she darted out into the middle of Auburn Street and took off like a bullet straight down the road.

Without thinking, and without any concern for my own safety (youthful ignorance, not courage, mind you), I chased after her as fast as my two legs could compete against her four. It was winter, remember, and the snow banks were piled up high along the sides of Auburn Street. I chased after Mandy into the road without so much as checking to see if even a bicycle was coming—in either direction! It would have been a fruitless gesture at any rate because, as I remember it, I couldn't see clearly over the snow banks anyway. All I remember hearing as I foolishly and recklessly dashed onto one of the busiest streets in Portland was, "Christopher! Don't chase her!"

Little did I know that my mother had witnessed what was happening from the window inside the house. It was her voice I heard. Instinctively I knew what I was doing was wrong because my mother never called me Christopher unless I was being accused of something or was in real trouble for some reason. At any rate she dashed out of the house too. As I ran, I remember my right arm raised high and shouting out, "Man-dy!" I thought for sure that this was it and that a moving car or truck would instantly kill my family's dog, and that it would be my fault entirely. I can't begin to describe the range of emotions I felt coursing through my adrenaline-soaked mind and body at that particular moment. It was truly frightening. What was even more frightening was that a car, turning onto Auburn Street, came up behind Mandy. From my vantage point in the middle of the road, it wasn't clear to me if the driver had seen her or not. Fortunately, the car's rear brake lights came on, and Mandy darted to the side of the road.

As luck would have it, besides that one turning car, there wasn't any traffic in the immediate area at that exact moment. Mandy (and I for that matter) could have been killed instantly by an oncoming vehicle the second we rounded the corner of the snow bank and onto the street. Fortunately the road was clear and we both were spared the vehicular wrath of Auburn Street. (A fate one of our cats did not escape, unfortunately.) I eventually caught up to Mandy down the road and was able to get my hands on her collar. I put my middle finger through the loop and pulled her collar tight. By this point, traffic had picked up and I had to wait a few seconds by the roadside until it was safe to lead her back home. My mother, frenzied and furious, met us in the driveway. I don't clearly remember what was said, but I got a good tongue-lashing from her. At that point I think I was still unaware of the severity and stupidity of my actions. It sank in later—believe me. For a brief time, I feared my mother would feed me nothing but her Hamburger Pie as punishment! Mandy, as usual, had no clue how much trouble she had caused. I can only imagine her sleeping soundly that night knowing she had gotten the better of me and that she had gotten an unexpected taste of freedom that evening, which no doubt made her very happy.

Mandy was quirky. There's no questioning that point. All dogs are to an ex- tent I suppose, but Mandy did some truly odd things. If you'll allow me to venture into the realm of the disgusting briefly, I'll share a few of her peculiar and less refined qualities. First off, as I've touched on before, Mandy was an eating machine. She would try to consume anything that passed her sniff inspection. She ate well. Not only did she get her own food, but also she got a lot of treats, table scraps, and big beef bones to gnaw on. At times she would devour her food so quickly that her stomach was overwhelmed, and as fast as she got it down, she would puke it all right back up either onto the floor or directly back into her bowl. And as if that wasn't bad enough, without a second's hesitation, she would scarf down the regurgitated mess almost as fast as when it was consumed the first time! It's also worth mentioning that

Mandy would frequently drink out of the toilet bowl. A habit she was never fully broken of.

Mandy would defiantly go after food put down for our cats. She'd shove them out of the way and gobble down their meals unless someone was there to guard it. Mandy was indifferent to our cats. She never chased them to speak of and as clear as I can remember, never scuffled with them either—at least not in the typical way people envision dogs and cats fighting. It was definitely not an archetypal "dog vs. cat" relationship. For the most part, they ignored one another, which I was happy to see but always thought was odd. Again, in mentioning the family cats, I'll point out that all of them were terrified of going to the vet. Every one of them would meow and tremble once they were loaded into the car and carted off to the vet's office. It was as if they knew exactly where they were going and what was happening—and they dreaded it. Mandy, on the other hand, leaped at the opportunity to get in the car and go to the vet. She loved going there and being around other animals. Did she behave? Mostly not, but the visit to the vet was exciting to her and she had no problems getting up on the examination table and being jabbed with syringes, fed heartworm pills, or receiving flea and tick treatments. Seeing how our cats reacted to the vet, I always thought Mandy's excitement when going there was a bit strange.

Mandy was very easily excitable. It generally didn't take a lot to get her riled up. However, there was one thing that would absolutely put her into a crazed frenzy whenever she was exposed to it. What was that one thing you ask? In one word, "fireworks." First let me state that lighting off fireworks in the city of Portland has been illegal dating back to the catastrophic Portland fire of 1866. However, the law is widely ignored by many Portland residents every Fourth of July. As luck would have it, one year my father came into possession of a large and impressive box of illegal fireworks from a friend of his. For years, he resisted my constant pleading to light them off. However, on the Fourth of July in 1986, my parents had a little party in the backyard, which included old friends from Lester Drive and lots of swimming fun for the kids. When it got dark enough, my father broke out the box of fireworks and allowed us kids to help set them off. Mandy was taken inside the house so she'd be out of danger and out of the way. Well, as soon as the show started, Mandy went wild barking and racing throughout the house. As we lit off bottle rockets, roman candles, and strings of firecrackers, Mandy went berserk. Even though she was inside, the noise and the bright explosions sent her into a fit. When the show was over, I remember going inside and watching my mother try to calm Mandy down. She was still barking and shaking out of what I would assume was both excitement and fear. If I remember correctly, I think she even wet the rug. It was a while before she was settled down, and we never lit off fireworks in our back yard again after that. As much as I loved the Fourth of July and fireworks, I felt bad that night.

Some other quirky qualities Mandy had involved her hygiene—for lack of a better way of saying it. She didn't mind being dirty, or wet for that matter. In fact I think she seemed happier when she was soaked and covered in mud. She certainly didn't mind the rain, as it was common to see her pacing back and forth on her run while it was pouring out. Rarely did one find her seeking refuge in her dry doghouse during a shower. As for the mud, Mandy spent a great deal of time outdoors and would regularly be caked in mud from her belly down to her claws. She hated the tub and being bathed in general. I nearly put my life at risk one time as a child when I stupidly got the bright idea that it would be a nice surprise for my parents if I gave Mandy a bath. Getting her into the tub was hard enough, but what happened afterwards was much worse. She growled and snarled at me, but I eventually got her in and wetted down. I soaped her up and did my best to clean her scruffy, black coat. Of course she hopped out before I could properly rinse or dry her off, and she proceeded to exit the bathroom and get the rug and walls all wet when she shook to dry herself. I was eventually able to towel her off, but she was still damp and slowly began to emanate that awful "wet dog" smell. My parents were none too thrilled at the state of the bathtub either. It was now filthy and the drain was clogged with dog hair. Overall it was a bad idea that didn't make anyone happy. Youthful good intentions are the only defense I can offer.

Another thing Mandy hated was to be lifted off the ground. Every time I tried to pick her up she'd growl and squirm to get away from me.

My mother, on the other hand, had the magic touch. If she picked Mandy up, there was no sign of resistance whatsoever. She wouldn't bark, growl, or squirm. At best, she'd muster a little whimper, but nothing more intense than that. I guess she knew that it was not wise to bite the hand that fed her. I give her credit for that!

There's one last enduring story about Mandy that needs to be told here. Although it occurred nearly thirty years ago, (from the time I write this, that is), it is still very fresh in my mind, partially because of what happened, and partially because the whole incident was captured and preserved on videotape. In the summer of 1988, my father purchased a VHS camcorder from Sears. As was common in those days, the camera was a big, clunky thing that rested on your shoulder while you looked through a viewfinder and recorded something. I fell in love with it instantly, and there was nothing I liked to do more than make home movies. The camcorder was glued to my shoulder that whole summer and there was next to nothing happening in the Morin household that I didn't capture on tape.

On one sunny day, I happened to be in the back yard filming nothing of real significance. My mother was tending her clothesline and Mandy was tied up as usual. All of a sudden, she burst out into a barking fit. I swung the camera around and began taping the commotion. My mother came over and we both witnessed Mandy squaring off with a brazen woodchuck that had entered her territory. Mandy barked, growled and danced around the animal like Muhammad Ali in his prime. But, staying true to form, Mandy's aggressive posturing was nothing more than an elaborate act staged for the cameras—in this case, quite literally. The woodchuck held its ground and didn't move a muscle. I couldn't tell if it was acting bravely or just bored by Mandy's silly act of aggression. The action intensified when Mandy got a little to close and the woodchuck nipped her snout. Mandy whined and retreated but kept up her barking. My mother, having seen enough, ordered me to put the camera down and rescue the dog. I brought Mandy in the house, her wound not serious. (Thankfully the woodchuck was not rabid.) She would carry that scar for the rest of her life and I would keep the videotape of the less than epic battle she fought with the woodchuck that day. It still gets viewed on occasion in my house—even today.

Time passed, as time always does, and the eighties were quickly giving way to the nineties. I was in high school now and my brother was starting college. Mandy was getting older too. Her chin now had lots of grayish-white hairs beneath it, as did other parts of her body. She was noticeably slower and less rambunctious, and her legs (particularly her hind ones) were gradually weakening as evidenced by her subtle discomfort when rising to her feet. More and more she began to use her forelegs to pull her up rather than her hind legs to push her up. Over time, Mandy increasingly kept to areas of the house that had carpet and did her best to avoid the slick hardwood floors. One Thanksgiving holiday, while everyone was celebrating and laughing in the kitchen, I heard a meek whimper coming from my parents' bedroom. Upon investigation, I found Mandy looking like a baby deer stranded on an icy pond. Her hind legs had given out on the hardwood floor and were nearly parallel to the ground as if she were trying to do a split. She was in trouble and obviously in pain. I rushed over and swiftly pulled her hind end up so her legs could straighten out and support her weight. She left the room without hesitation. She wanted to get carpet under her paws as fast as she could.

It's never easy to witness a beloved pet's decline. As the years wear on, it's typically the body that starts to break down first where dogs are concerned. Mandy was no exception. Although very gradual, it was her hind legs that began to initially and noticeably fail. She began to hesitate whenever confronted with a slick surface and eventually stairs became a tremendous burden for her. Slowly, her world began to shrink, and it only got smaller as she grew older.

Suffice it to say, despite Mandy's physical weakening, her mind remained as foolish and energetic as ever. (Unfortunately I can't claim that her intelligence increased with age.) She never passed up an opportunity to go outside, ride in the car, or snatch up a treat when people weren't looking. She still possessed a youthful exuberance that never waned.

Throughout my high school years, my relationship with Mandy changed. I became more of a caregiver to her than a playmate. I went from shirking responsibility for her to taking more responsibility for her. She needed more care and assistance as she aged, and for the first time in my life I truly began to realize that she wouldn't be around forever. We still were a team in many respects—she secretly continued to help me clean my plate well into my late teens—and we still had fun together, even if it was just simple games of "scratch my belly." Unfortunately, her ability to fetch tennis balls or play tug-of-war was long gone.

My mother, as always, had the largest burden. She was unquestionably the primary caregiver and provider for Mandy. She spent the most time with her during the day and watched after her unfailingly. As time passed, Mandy spent less time tied up in the back yard and more time in the house under my mother's watchful eye. I began to notice that Mandy spent increasing amounts of time riding in the car during her twilight years. Occasionally my furry little friend would be riding shotgun when my mother picked me up from school. It was a treat for her and less of a worry for my mother as I'm sure she didn't like leaving Mandy home alone in those days.

I graduated from Deering High School in the spring of 1992. My college destination was the University of Maine at Orono, where my older brother was currently being schooled. By this time, Mandy was very near the end of her life. Amazingly, though her physical limitations restricted her movements, she was remarkably spry and still capable of moving independently without the aid of others. And if you put food in front of her, particularly a favorite treat such as Smartfood popcorn, she'd spring to life as if she were a puppy again. She was a tough old girl. There's no questioning that fact.

Throughout my first year of college, my brother and I would travel back and forth from Orono to Portland during school vacations. My brother had an old blue Chevy S-10 pickup truck that spent more time in the shop than on the road. Each time we returned home with stories from school and piles of dirty laundry, we'd find out how Mandy was doing. Most times she was fine as could be expected, while occasionally there'd be a story about her becoming slightly ill or having an accident on the floor. Every once in a while her legs would buckle and she'd fall over. I'd try to spend a good deal of time with her when I was home. Though I knew better, I still couldn't quite fully grasp the fact that her life was coming to an end—and that end would sadly be much sooner than later.

Sometime in the late autumn of 1992, Mandy was stricken with a neurological disorder called vestibular nystagmus, which affects the inner ear and ultimately balance. One morning my mother found Mandy collapsed on the floor surrounded by piles of vomit. Her eyes were spinning like tops and she was unable to stand. My parents rushed her to the vet where she was treated and eventually released. Upon returning home from school, my brother and I were briefed on what had happened and we noticed that Mandy's head was constantly tilted and she walked as if on a slant. She had recovered from her illness, but it had left her looking a bit cock-eyed. It was quite comical to witness and I spent many hours playfully teasing her and trying to "screw her head on straight." The good news was that she was okay and out of imminent danger.

One humorous story that I recall happened near the end of her life. It sums up all that Mandy was about on many levels and still brings smiles to my family's faces even to this day. My brother and I had come home from school during Christmas vacation in 1992. For many years, my parents' house has been the epicenter of festivities for the maternal side of my family. Each year the various members of my family converge on Auburn Street to celebrate major holidays, birthdays, and other events of significance. Christmas of 1992 went off normally like many before it. There was a substantial layer of snow on the ground that year and the night was chilly to say the least. It got dark quickly as the late afternoon approached. Sometime after dinner my father was given the task of walking Mandy out back so she could relieve herself. By this time in her life, Mandy spent almost all her time in the house and was rarely tied up outside all day like she had been in the past. Her mobility was significantly reduced to a very slow shuffle and she was definitely unable to run anymore. Her choke collar was all but abolished, and there was really no need for a leash anymore. My father escorted the slow-moving dog into the back yard. It was very dark and there was only one outside light, which poorly illuminated the immediate surroundings. Some time slipped by and everyone was surprised to see my father come back into the house without the dog. He went for his flashlight and casually, somewhat embarrassed, announced, "The dog got away from me."

We were all stunned. Mandy was virtually crippled and had somehow managed to sneak off while my father wasn't paying attention. Up until the very end of her life, that fire to run free was never extinguished from her failing mind and body. Amazing—I thought it then and still do today. For what was most certainly the last time, my family formed a posse to ensnare and recover our fugitive dog. We fanned out and set up a dragnet to bring home our wayward pet. Fortunately the search didn't take long and Mandy was discovered in the woods not far from where she made her initial escape. She was brought back into the safety and warmth of the house and we couldn't help but rib my father about the whole experience for the rest of the night. An old, senile, and decrepit dog had outwitted him just as she had outwitted me years earlier. Fortunately this time she didn't run onto Auburn Street!

One endearing image I remember vividly involving Mandy happened in the spring of 1993. It was a sunny day, and my brother and I were leaving Auburn Street to head back up to Orono after some time off. As we were backing out of the driveway, my mother and Mandy stood side by side and waved goodbye. My mother knelt down and picked up one of Mandy's paws and waved it at us so it looked liked Mandy herself was waving goodbye. It was a simple gesture, but one that has stuck with me to this day.

Sadly, the end came in the fall of 1993. I had just started my sophomore year at UMO and was looking forward to coming home for Columbus Day weekend. Before my brother and I left campus, I got a phone call from my mother who was audibly upset. She was in tears and I immediately thought the worst when she mentioned Mandy. To my relief she hadn't expired, but my mother explained that she was no longer able to stand and she didn't know what to say or do. I reassured her the best I could, and my brother and I returned home as quickly as possible.

Upon arrival at Auburn Street, we both immediately went to our dog's side. She was quiet and subdued. I patted her and told her how happy I was to see her. I tried to help her to her feet, but it was a forgone conclusion—she couldn't stand up anymore. That night the family ordered Chinese food from the Wok-Inn. I sat on the floor next to Mandy and secretly fed her, like I had done my whole life, but this time just for fun. The last thing I ever saw her eat was a piece of beef teriyaki from my hand.

That night the family discussed what to do, but none of us could suggest putting her down. It was too painful to say. The next day, Mandy worsened. There comes a time when animals sense that the end is near and they just give up. They stop eating, drinking, and generally become unresponsive to anything or anyone. They crawl into a corner, lie down, and just wait to die. Sadly, Mandy was no exception. We placed a tarp underneath her in the sunken living room and tried to make her as comfortable as possible. No decision was made on what to do then, but my father arranged to take me to the movies that night. The film *Gettysburg* had just been released, and my father knew that I was a big fan of Civil War history. He and I went to see the four-hour film that evening. At appropriate times we discussed what should be done with Mandy. As much as it pained me to say it, I suggested she be put down the next day to spare her any further pain or discomfort. She had already stopped eating and it was only a matter of time before she truly began to suffer. He agreed, and that was the true beginning of the end.

The next day my father spent the morning making arrangements for Mandy's final act. Once everything was set, neither my brother nor I wanted to witness it. My brother made plans with friends and I promised my grandmother that I'd go over to her house and trim her hedges for her. Before I left, however, I knelt down next to my dying dog and patted her gently. I whispered in her ear and told her how much I loved her and how happy I was that she was a part of my life. I then said my final goodbye to our beloved pet. I stormed out the front door and headed to my grandmother's house. That was the final time I saw Mandy. (As I remember that day, and as I write this now, there are tears streaming down my face.)

Mandy was euthanized and cremated. Her ashes are preserved in a special box that resides on my parents' fireplace mantel to this day. To try and sum up the full impact she had on my life would be futile; however, there are some vital points that must be said here and now. She was my family's first dog, and she holds a special place in my heart for that one simple reason alone. She was a part of my life from the time I was four until I was nineteen. We played together, we ate together, we got into trouble together, and we learned about life together. In a sense, we grew up together. Mandy was by far the naughtiest, most reckless, and most incorrigible dog my family ever owned. She did things that other families wouldn't have tolerated and would have most likely gotten her sent to a pound. She skirted death on more than one occasion and ended up living the longest of any of the animals my family ever possessed. At times her life was hard, but she had a loving family that was able to continually overlook her shortcomings. And though we often tend to dwell on the more annoying and destructive times of her life, we can't ever forget the good times and the joy she brought to our young family.

Even today, though she's been gone for twenty-three years, I still think of her often, and occasionally she visits me in my dreams. Sometimes she's old and sometimes she's young. Sometimes I'm old and sometimes I'm young. But the one thing that's always constant is that she and I are always happy to see each other and cause a little mischief, the way we did together so many years ago. Sometimes the dreams are vague, while other times they're extremely vivid. Sometimes they're powerful enough where I find myself waking up in tears. Only now can I understand just how much she meant to me…my beloved "Pupster," a nickname I gave her a long time ago. Fortunately my family is blessed with lots of pictures and old mementoes of that dog. They will undoubtedly be treasured until all who knew her are gone. Though she was born in the late seventies and lived until the early nineties, Mandy will always be remembered as our dog of the eighties. She lived for fifteen years—and what a wild ride those years were!

MEMORIES

MANDY PHOTOGRAPHS

Mandy in her later years.

Yours truly 4, and my brother 7, with our new puppy, Mandy.

Mandy by the "Hamburger Hassock," with my hand and foot in the background.

Mandy as a young pup on my father's lap.

Mandy lying in wait by my empty chair, hoping for some Hamburger Pie.

Chewed tools still in my father's workshop.

Close-up of chewed hammer end.

Close-up of chewed saw handle.

Sole surviving Star Wars Jawa.
Notice the chewed right shoulder.

Chewed Lego toys from the 70s & 80s still in my possession today.

At "The Lot." Mandy in the foreground and me on my bike in the background.

Trees cleared and logs stacked at "The Lot." Old Chevy van to the right with chainsaw visible.

Me, my brother, and Mandy exploring "The Lot" for the first time circa 1980.

Entrance to "The Lot" as it looks today. Compare it to the older images.

Mandy and yours truly playing fetch on Sand Island, July 1985.

More Sand Island fun with yours truly and my aquatic loving dog, Mandy.

Mandy emerging from her doghouse on Auburn Street circa 1990.

Lester Drive house circa 1984. Notice Mandy's dog house at far right.

My mother posing a "less than enthusiastic" Mandy for the camera circa 1992.

Mandy leashed out back of Auburn Street.

Yours truly, my brother and Mandy, Christmas 1991. All three of us look a lot different than we did on the steps in 1978!

An aged Mandy near the end of her life.

CHAPTER TWO

TRUCKER

Trucker was his name. Born in a place called North Pole, Alaska, one might wonder just exactly how this dog—a purebred black Lab—journeyed clear across the country and found a new home in Portland, Maine. Well, as much as I'd like to build up the suspense, the story is not that complicated. However, it is a bit intriguing nevertheless.

It was late in the spring of 1994—June to be precise. Mandy had been gone for several months now and my mother, though never one to broadcast sad emotions, was somewhat distraught at the absence of a dog in our household. I witnessed her on more than one occasion involuntarily reach down with food scraps as she trimmed meat or peeled vegetables at the kitchen sink, thinking Mandy was right there and would chomp down the food as she had done so many times before. Only now my mother had to sadly pull her hand back up, remembering Mandy wasn't there. Though she rarely discussed Mandy's absence, it clearly affected her. Yes, my mother, once a bona fide cat person, had grown to admire canines—specifically black Labs. In fairness, though her attitude had shifted to favor dogs and her appreciation for the companionship they provided was evident, neither my mother nor my father had any intentions of seeking out a new four-legged pet at that time. However, little did they know that a scheme had been hatched to introduce a new black dog into their lives.

Trucker was born in 1988. Ironically, he was owned by the son of the woman, (Kathy Waldron), who had brought Mandy into our home. The son, named Burke, was a state trooper in Alaska, having moved and gone to school there years earlier. His father, a longtime friend and frequent visitor of my parents, helped put together a plan that would bring Trucker to Maine and into my mother's heart.

At the time, Burke was married with a young son and a pregnant wife. His job as a trooper forced him and his family to relocate throughout the state quite frequently. Oftentimes, finding lodgings (either very temporary or semi-permanent) that allowed dogs was difficult. So after taking these simple truths into account and then factoring in some unknowns, the situation was ripe for the Alaskan Waldron family to pull off a masterful plan that was not only overly generous beyond all expectations, but beneficial for all parties involved. In simpler language, Burke and his family presented my mother with a convenient problem that would change her life for the better.

As the story goes, Burke and his wife Janet proposed that they needed to find a "temporary" home for Trucker as they were going to be moving to a place that didn't allow dogs. I'm sure there was much more to it than that, but I was away at college at the time and was not privy to the initial conversations and arrangements made. Essentially, my mother agreed to take care of the dog, and in early June of 1994 the Waldrons boarded a plane with a crated Trucker, and flew to Maine.

As I understood it at the time, Trucker was to be kept and cared for by my parents for maybe a year or so until Burke and his family settled in a spot where all the right requirements were met for his family and the dog. Under the circumstances, it was a convincing story—to say the least. But over time, it became readily apparent to *me* that Burke had no intention of ever retrieving Trucker, and that he fully intended to give him to my mother outright under false yet harmless and very generous pretenses.

This is speculation on my part, as I have never thoroughly discussed the matter with all the parties involved, nor was I ever part of the plan, but in my opinion my mother's melancholy state after Mandy's death was conveniently and most assuredly relayed to Burke via his father who, as I mentioned earlier, was a regular visitor to my parents' household. The beginnings of the idea originated there in my opinion. The timing and circumstances surrounding the Waldron family problems were logical and fell into place, making a great cover story. They would plan to give their dog to my mother, knowing full well that there wasn't a better place on earth to send him except into her hands. Again, that is simply how *I* perceived the chain of events as they unfolded. The unmitigated truth may in fact be slightly different and may never be completely revealed. For now, however, there isn't any more to be discussed concerning that particular issue. So, for the second time in my family's history, the generosity of a Waldron produced a Morin family pet. In June of 1994, Trucker became that pet.

Unfortunately I must state that Trucker's portion of this narrative will undoubtedly be the shortest. This is in no way meant to slight him of his due credit; however, the simple fact is, of the three dogs we owned, he was around the shortest period of time—just eight years. And in those eight years, I lived at Auburn Street for only a very short stint. When Trucker arrived I was halfway through college and thus not living at home during the school year. When I graduated in 1996, I lived at home for only a little over a year before I purchased my first house (in Portland, by the way) in the fall of 1997. I must also state that when I was home I worked third shift at a local Hannaford store (called Shop 'n' Save at the time) and slept most of the day in the summertime. All these factors combined to hinder my daily interaction with Trucker, though I do have many interesting and amusing stories to impart from the time we did spend together.

Trucker was a full-grown purebred black Lab, age six, when he first arrived in Maine. He had a very deep and masculine bark that sharply contrasted to what I had grown accustomed to hearing from Mandy. He looked like a very typical black Lab. His coat was shorthaired and solid black. He was lean with a rugged build, and he had powerful legs for both running and jumping. His head was kind of square shaped with floppy ears, and he had a long snout. Curiously, one of his physical features that stuck out in my mind was his tongue. Upon seeing it, you'd swear it was as long as a snake and as wide as a Ping-Pong paddle. To me, it seemed to hang right down to the floor every time he would pant. His tongue was infamous in some ways and I'll share more about it a bit later; however, I will say now that my first introduction with Trucker thoroughly involved his tongue. When I first met the dog, I was fresh home from college and the Waldrons had just arrived in

Portland. They brought him over to Auburn Street with his crate, red plaid L.L. Bean bed, water and food dishes, and leash. He scurried into the house at full speed intent on thoroughly checking out his new surroundings. When his interests shifted to me, I knelt down beside him in order to give him a good welcome pat on the head. He proceeded to knock me over on my back, jump onto my chest, and lick my face unlike anything I had ever experienced. When he finished, I felt like a washcloth drenched in dog saliva had repeatedly been dragged across my visage. I had never been given such a lovable yet completely disgusting welcome!

One interesting tidbit I remember from Trucker's first few weeks with us was that it coincided with the infamous O.J. Simpson white Bronco chase that was televised live and widely broadcast at the time. It was late in the evening (in Maine that is) and I was getting ready to go to work. I remember standing by the door and watching the action unfold on TV. Trucker was nearby and appeared just as interested in what was happening on the set as I was. Ironically, my mother was on the phone talking to the Waldrons, who had just returned home to Alaska and were inquiring how Trucker was behaving. Now, every time I'm reminded of that famous chase, I always think of him.

It didn't take long for us to realize that Trucker was unlike Mandy in many ways. The most obvious difference was his intelligence. He was very smart and exceptionally well trained before arriving in Maine. He could do a whole series of tricks and was very adept at obeying orders on command. He knew how to speak, sit, lie down, roll over, and come when his named was called. He was completely housebroken and had a funny way of telling you when he needed to go out. When the time came, Trucker would go into my parents' bedroom and retrieve a single shoe or slipper. He'd then find the nearest human and drop the footwear at their feet. That was his way of telling you that he needed to go out and do his duty. As neat as that was, the coolest trick I ever saw him do involved a treat. We'd take a Milk-Bone and place it on the end of his rather prominent snout. He'd sit there frozen like a statue until someone gave him the command, "Okay!" At that point, he'd flip the treat up off his nose and catch it in his mouth almost without fail. As you can imagine, it was quickly devoured.

Trucker possessed intelligence that I believe often caught my family off guard, sometimes pleasantly, other times annoyingly. Up to that point I had never experienced having a dog that minded on command. He was not destructive like Mandy was and never caused any damage throughout the house. He could be left alone for hours without fear of chewing the place up or injuring himself. He was generally a pretty cool customer and didn't have frenzied meltdowns like Mandy did in her early years. He was certainly unique in many ways and less trouble due to his earlier training.

Despite all his admirable qualities, which were a breath of fresh air, Trucker was far from perfect. He did possess many naughty characteristics that would frequently get him in trouble. For the first year or so living at Auburn Street, Trucker was generally well behaved. But soon after, he went through a rebellious phase where he took every opportunity to take off and explore the neighborhood—shades of Mandy. First I must back up a bit and convey that Trucker was the bridge between the old style and the more modern style of dog care my family experienced/practiced at the time. In the beginning, Trucker was leashed like Mandy. In fact, he was tied up out back on Mandy's old dog trolley run that had never been taken down. Her old doghouse was still in place too. Trucker didn't wear a choke collar. He had a more modern conventional collar that was blue, which became his unofficial signature color.

When put out in the morning and tied to the dog trolley, Trucker would rebel by barking loudly and nonstop. It got so bad that my parents began getting complaints from the neighbors because of the noise. That was interesting in and of itself because, unlike Lester Drive, the Auburn Street residence had only a few houses even remotely close to it and there was a decent tree buffer between them. I never witnessed this barking act of his because I was still in college, but I heard the stories from my parents during the occasional phone call. It got to the point where Trucker would routinely slip his collar and escape the dog trolley to go off and explore. One time he pulled the whole aging apparatus down with nothing but brute strength and a desire to be free. When that happened, that was the end of not only the dog trolley, but the end of trying to keep him contained and restrained. The old style of keeping your dog tied up in the yard while you got on with your day was over and a new one was emerging.

Trucker came from Alaska and was used to a more unrestricted type of freedom that the great rural stretches of that land provided. He was used to more mobility and less restrictions on his movements. He did not like to be chained or leashed in any way. Reminiscent of Mandy, he too would try to pull your arm out of the socket whenever you tried to take him for a walk on his leash. To fix that problem, my mother got him a special harness, (a type you see used quite commonly today), that fit around his upper torso and restricted his ability to pull without choking his neck. It worked and he responded much better to it. He would also stop pulling (temporarily) if you commanded him to heel.

Unfortunately, the dangers of a loose dog in and around Auburn Street were still evident—particularly being struck and killed by a car. The reality was that Trucker came from a place with many fewer automobiles, and a smaller chance of being killed by one, to a place where traffic streamed by virtually nonstop and the risk of being hit was much greater. My mother and father had to find a way to accommodate his desire to be free but, at the same time, protect him from the dangers he was unaware of.

Trucker proved in the beginning that he would not immediately bolt the second he was unleashed and outside like Mandy would. He could be let outside without a leash and would faithfully remain by your side—for the most part. One thing he loved to do was to play Frisbee. Often my father or I would take Trucker out back and fling the Frisbee for him. He'd chase it down and leap high into the air to catch it before running it back to you to fling again. This activity was good because it gave him the exercise and attention that Labs desire, but also extended him the freedom he craved. Only sometimes he'd chase down the Frisbee and just keep going off into the woods or out onto the road.

When Trucker was feeling feisty, and had the opportunity, he'd go for it and just take off. This used to put my mother into a panic because she knew he had no fear of cars and wasn't overly familiar with his surroundings, thus increasing his risk of being injured or killed. There was no catching him when he took off. The best my mother could do was drive around the neighborhood, hope to find him, and pray he would obey the command to come. Sometimes she would find him, and sometimes he would return to the car on command, but more often than not she wouldn't find him and would simply have to drive home to wait. Most of the time he would return home on his own accord unscathed. Frequently however, my mother would get a phone call from a neighbor or acquaintance saying they had him and could she please come pick him up.

Trucker liked to get into other people's garbage, and he also would stop to play with other neighborhood dogs in their yards. One time my mother tracked him down in a neighbor's yard frolicking with some new four-legged friends. She claims he saw her coming and, like a defiant child, quickly hid behind a bush to evade capture! Fortunately, during those early rebellious times, Trucker always made it home unharmed. A miraculous feat if you're at all familiar with the traffic on Auburn Street.

Over time, Trucker learned to behave, and his bolting became more infrequent and eventually stopped. Soon the everyday focus was more on his positive qualities rather than his negative ones, and my mother's affection for him grew with each passing day. He really wasn't a "family pet," like Mandy was, as my brother and I were never home and my father was at work all day. He essentially became "my mother's dog," since she was around him the most and took care of him. She started to take him with her wherever she went. She drove an SUV and conveniently set up the back area to comfortably house Trucker as he rode with her. He'd leap into the car on cue after hearing the command "mount up" from whoever was chauffeuring him at the time. My mother frequently took him for walks in the park, to the beach, and various other places; and he was all too happy to go with her. (Trucker did have one annoying quality while in the car. He whined nonstop when the vehicle was in motion. We never could figure out why, but the whining persisted until the very end.) In time, my mother rarely if ever left the house without taking *her* dog with her.

My mother and Trucker became almost inseparable. She had a dog to mother and spoil like a child, and he had a caregiver who gave him the very best of attention. This was the time when Trucker became "humanized," as is mostly the norm today. My mother bought him all kinds of toys and started feeding him more expensive types of dog food. He had comfortable dog beds to sleep on and was even allowed up on the furniture from time to time—primarily when my father wasn't around. His picture was taken frequently and professionally, and even a small painting was rendered of him by his former human mother, Janet, and given to my mother.

One of the most enjoyable and entertaining spectacles to behold involving Trucker was when we had parties or were celebrating an occasion/holiday that involved wrapped presents. Trucker never went without, and even if the occasion wasn't specifically about him, he always got his share of presents. The interesting part was not what he got, but what he did with what he got. Put simply, Trucker loved to open wrapped presents. He would get excited and jump up and down (he had an extraordinary vertical leap, by the way) or dance about until you placed his present in front of him. His tail would thump on the floor at a dizzying speed causing what felt like a minor, localized, earthquake. The second the present was placed at his feet, his ears would perk up and his eyes would lock on you...but he wouldn't open the present—just yet. He waited for the command "get it," whereupon he would pounce on the package and start shredding the exterior wrapping paper with a combined frontal assault involving his teeth and his front claws. Seconds later, the paper would be nothing more than hundreds of small colored shreds scattered across the floor with whatever it formally concealed now firmly resting between his upper and lower jaws.

He could open presents all day—he loved them—and he always put on a great show for everyone watching. Believe me, Trucker knew how to draw a crowd and he soaked up all the additional attention. One time, back in Alaska, his penchant for opening presents got him in trouble—sort of. The Waldrons had wrapped up a new bed for him and put it under the Christmas tree. Either he was told the present was for him or he simply figured it out on his own. Nevertheless, the next morning, to the Waldron's surprise, Trucker had pulled his gift out from under the tree, unwrapped it himself, and was happily asleep on his new bed!

Trucker just had a style that was all his own. He carried himself with a peculiar type of coolness and swagger that often made you wonder if he was actually human and just masquerading as a dog. His intelligence and uncanny ability to understand what you commanded him to do was—at times—astonishing in my opinion. I always felt that he understood what you required of him, and if he didn't obey, it wasn't because he didn't understand the command; it was because he simply didn't feel like following your orders. Ignorance is a word I never widely associated with Trucker. He was quite clever. Though his intelligence made caring for him much easier, it also promoted lots of mischief. If you weren't paying attention, at any given moment, that dog could outwit you.

Trucker had a wild side to him when it came to other animals. He'd chase squirrels up trees and dig huge holes in the ground going after woodchucks, chipmunks, or any other small mammal he thought he could get at. Birds were no safer. Coming from Alaska and being owned by an avid hunter, Trucker was undoubtedly and routinely exposed to a plethora of wildlife unlike those most common pets experience in their lifetimes—winged or otherwise. What he saw in Maine most likely dulled in comparison to what he normally tangled with in Alaska, but it certainly didn't kill his spirit.

An interesting little bird story involved a stuffed white ptarmigan that was given to my parents by the Waldrons as a present and mounted on our wall. Trucker generally paid no attention to it until someone randomly and casually asked, "Trucker, where's the bird?" At that point, he would hurry over to the spot on the wall where it was mounted and stare at it intently while emanating short whines and rocking back and forth in an excited state. It was truly fun to watch, and I think the simple game brought out the hunter/retriever traits in him. At that point, you'd have to get his mind on something else before he'd stop carrying on about the ptarmigan. I always found food to be the most enticing remedy—and so did Trucker.

Another story that involved Trucker and birds happened in a vacant lot in South Portland where my mother, and occasionally yours truly, would take him for exercise. This particular lot was abandoned and fenced in, so it provided an ideal place to take the dog when he needed a quick run. The drill was simple: Let Trucker out of the car, guide him into the enclosure, sit back, and watch him run around. When he became tired or bored, he'd hustle back and let you know he was ready to go. Only one time, there were a bunch of pigeons poking around inside the fence. My mother had him that day and never gave a thought to the portly group of birds scrounging around in the corner. Trucker, on the other hand, had other ideas. He darted after the pigeons like a wolf after a rabbit. My mother was not concerned as she was quite sure he'd never catch one—boy, was she wrong! Within minutes, Trucker had pounced on one, killed it, and brought the bloody bird back to my mother as if she were a hunter and he was simply retrieving game for her. Horrified, my mother got the bird away from him and tried to dispose of it. But no matter where she placed it, Trucker went after it and continued to bring it back to her! Finally she got the two separated and was able to get Trucker in the car. From that day on, I'm sure she was wary of what he was capable of doing when in the presence of wild animals—and planned more accordingly.

Despite some of his rougher qualities, Trucker was really a very lovable dog. When he wasn't feeling sassy or getting into trouble, he loved to be patted and smothered with attention. In return, he'd snuggle right up to you and oftentimes cover your hands (or your face, if you'd let him) with several big licks from that massive tongue of his. He would stay faithfully at your side and thump his tail hard on the floor to express his contentment. Trucker, like most Labs, never liked being alone and would pout or sulk whenever he found himself without anyone around—particularly my mother. There was one time in 1995 when my parents went out to Alaska to visit with the Waldrons for a week or so. It was summer, and I was home from college. I was working my usual third shift at the supermarket, and my brother at the time was living out of town. Basically it was just Trucker, our one cat Lucy, and I holding down the fort. Because of my odd work schedule, I couldn't spend much time with Trucker, as I was asleep most of the day. We'd hang out in the evenings before I'd go to work, but it was very evident to me that he was sad, lonely, and missing my mother. I did my best. I walked, exercised, and played with him every chance I could. I took him to all his favorite spots and let him ride in the car with me whenever I went out to run an errand. We had some fun, but the most memorable part of that time spent with him happened one evening. I had the night off and got up early in the day so I could go to bed that night and have a normal day the next day. My bedroom was upstairs, and Trucker's bed was downstairs in our little TV viewing room next to my parents' bedroom. I remember locking up the house and turning off all the lights before going up to bed. Trucker was on his bed but not asleep. I gave him a pat on the head and went up to my room. I rarely, if ever, closed my bedroom door, and this evening was no exception. There was no moon that night, and I remember the house being exceptionally dark and quiet. Again, I thought nothing of it and went to sleep. The next thing I knew it was morning. I awoke to a surprise that I will never forget. Curled up in a big white ball at the end of my bed was our chubby cat, Lucy. This was not unusual, as Lucy often slept on my bed. However, what stunned me was the big *black* mass lying next to me. It was of course, Trucker, sound asleep. What makes this story even more interesting is that in those days I slept on a very uncomfortable twin-sized bed. How in the world both that dog and cat comfortably found room to climb up and share that bed with a six foot two, one hundred eighty-five-pound man is beyond my comprehension. What's even more interesting is that I had absolutely no idea when they climbed up or that they were even there until I woke up that morning. It truly was a strange sight. I wish someone could have taken a picture of it. Both animals were acting like a couple of small children who were afraid of the dark and afraid to be alone. You can imagine the joy Trucker experienced when he first saw my mother get out of the car after I picked everyone up from the airport a few days later.

Some old habits never die. Whenever I needed a little help disposing of some unwanted food at the dinner table, Trucker proved to be just as reliable as

Mandy. He became my new dinner table wingman. In speaking of food, Trucker certainly had a hearty appetite and would inhale most anything you fed him. He did, however, as I recall, have a much more sensitive stomach than his predecessor. He loved pig's ears and other rawhide treats, but sometimes they (and other foods) wouldn't agree with him and he'd become sick and puke. Burke's father (the person who frequently visited my parents' house) would routinely stuff him full of doughnuts and other baked goods that weren't the best for him. One particular food that's worth mentioning in reference to Trucker is Kentucky Fried Chicken. Occasionally my parents would enjoy some KFC takeout on the weekends. Aware of Trucker's sensitive stomach, they never fed him any of the fatty fowl. Before eating it, my father would typically remove all the skin, as he wasn't fond of all its greasiness or high calorie content. When the meal was over, all the waste, including the chicken skin, would go right into the trash. Well, you probably know where I'm heading with this—and you're right. Trucker got into the trash bucket and devoured all the chicken skin. However, the interesting part of this story is that it came back up almost as quickly as it went down! Whether he didn't like it or his stomach simply rejected it at light speed is still a mystery. What is fact is that the chicken skin barely had enough time to slide down his throat before the brakes were put on and the direction of the food sharply reversed!

Trucker had a habit of stealthily staking out the dinner table. Like a submerged submarine with its periscope raised, Trucker would linger under the table to the point where all you saw was the tip of his snout creep above the edge actively sniffing out a juicy morsel potentially within his range. Once his sniffer identified a target, he would deploy his primary and most reliable weapon—his tongue. Without hesitation and without warning, that massive pink oral appendage would erupt out of his mouth like a torpedo being launched from its tube. Whatever edible foodstuff lay in its reach was instantly and completely obliterated, showing little to no sign that it ever existed at all. Trucker would then submerge completely under the table until he deemed it safe to redeploy his periscope again. Once in a while someone would drop a verbal depth charge on him and he'd be chased out from under the murky depths of the dinner table and out into the open where he could more easily be observed.

Trucker's little periscope act was called "snorkeling" by the family. He'd "snorkel" around the table at mealtime, always on the lookout for dropped food. He begged at the table just like most dogs do. Unlike Mandy, however, Trucker didn't prance around and whine in hopes of getting a tasty handout. Trucker was much more sly and cunning. He rarely made any noise, and he looked for prime opportunities to snatch up some goodies rather than force himself on someone. "No wretched begging," was the command used to get him away from the table. The phrase had originated in Alaska with the Waldrons and had carried over to the Morins once Trucker was in Maine. It usually worked, and the dog would normally obey on command. Trucker usually set up shop near me, as he was more likely to get a treat from yours truly than anybody else. Needless to say, regardless if you felt like sharing or not, you always had to watch your plate when Trucker was around.

Trucker loved parties, not only for the presents, but also for the people there and for the cake. He had a thing for birthday cakes. Over time, my mother would prepare cakes that she knew he could safely eat. And when his birthday came around, he had his own special cake that oftentimes rivaled, if not exceeded, the opulence and size of the cakes bought or prepared for the human members of the family! He would gobble down most any baked good you put in front of him, but I believe he was especially fond of cakes…and particularly frosting. In one stroke, Trucker's tongue could strip a layer of frosting off a slice of cake faster than a windshield wiper set on high could wipe away the rain. I once heard a story about a birthday party thrown for him in Alaska where a freshly baked and frosted cake was prepared for him and set on the edge of the table. It wasn't long before that long pink tongue of his (and only the tongue) was seen stealthily and efficiently lapping the frosting clean from under the tabletop. It was a classic Trucker maneuver.

Trucker had it the worst when it came to physical injuries. His spirited nature got him hurt more than once. He badly cut his rear left paw one time while running at the vacant lot in South Portland. He limped back to the car on three legs leaving a trail of blood spots behind. The paw needed stitching and was bandaged up tightly by the vet.

Another time he got loose behind my parents' house and eventually came home with blood dripping from his chest. After closer inspection by the vet, it was surmised that he had slightly impaled himself on a sharp stick—or something of that nature—projecting out of the ground at just the right angle. He was patched up and acted no worse for the wear—that was Trucker. The injury did force him to wear a protective cone around his neck so he would be unable to bite at and loosen the stitches on his chest. I laughed heartily at first sight of him with his plastic cone that more resembled a cheap lampshade than anything else. I immediately nicknamed him "Nerd Dog." But Trucker being Trucker had the last laugh. He quickly learned to navigate through the woods smoothly while wearing the cone and at times even slipped out of it!

It wasn't only sharp objects that inflicted pain on my mother's dog, but also the native wildlife. Trucker occasionally mixed it up with local skunks, and once he really took a shellacking. One time, in broad daylight, Trucker went after a skunk in our back yard. The skunk let loose a torrent of spray that hit the dog squarely in the face. Wounded and unable to carry out his initial frontal assault, Trucker had to retreat, leaving the skunk victorious and in command of the battlefield. He hobbled back to the safety of the house, and my mother began nursing duties. Trucker's eyes watered like mad and he vomited from the spray. Naturally he stunk to high heavens, and my mother couldn't get the smell out even after repeated baths. What's more interesting is what happened the very next day. Trucker was let out to relieve himself, when he spotted the very same skunk still entrenched in his territory. Having no desire to leave the enemy in control of the field for two straight days, Trucker bolstered up his reserves and initiated another charge that would surely bring him a decisive victory over the invading enemy black-and-white-striped forces. However, a neutral entity intervened. My mother quickly hollered at the dog from her observation platform high above the field of battle (most likely the kitchen window) and stopped his charge. The skunk, realizing his weapons were depleted, and that he had limited reserves, hastily withdrew out of the war zone and into the safety of the woods. Trucker, though unable to savor the victory in the fashion he desired, had won the day and was again king of the back yard.

Though Trucker was a tough customer who always seemed to shrug off injury, there was one painful genetic characteristic he couldn't avoid. Like many black Lab purebreds, Trucker had inherited a physical degenerative trait in his hind hips and legs. As he got older, his hind joints got weaker as the cartilage and bone began to break down. In 1997, just three years after he arrived in Maine, my mother began to notice him limp more and more whenever she walked him. I'm sure she began to notice that a considerable amount of wind had been taken out of his sails also. (It was unlike Trucker to ever do anything at less than full throttle.) This prompted a visit to the vet, where he was diagnosed with hip dysplasia. The condition was advanced enough where he needed surgery to correct the problem.

Trucker underwent femoral head osteotomy surgery for his left hip. To be more precise, he underwent the surgical removal of the head and neck of the left femur. In even simpler language, the "ball" part of the ball-and-socket that made up the hip joint was removed. This relieved the pain and pressure caused by the hip and leg bones grinding against each other. Amazingly, once the procedure is complete, and the animal begins to heal, the surrounding muscles and developing scar tissue act to support the affected area and act as a false joint. In time, the animal's stricken limb strengthens and recovers a good portion if not the majority of its former mobility.

Poor Trucker. I remember seeing him at home looking all despondent and miserable. I'm sure he was in pain or some form of discomfort, but rarely did you ever hear him whimper or grumble. He could walk on his own, but his left leg hung limply like a strand of wet pasta. I couldn't help myself. Despite what he had gone through, I still had to tease him and aptly nicknamed him "Spaghetti Leg." Not very original or clever, but it certainly fit.

It didn't take long for Trucker's spirits to rise. I don't think God has ever created a more optimistic creature on this earth than a Labrador retriever.

Soon Trucker adapted to using only three legs. He began to walk and even run quite effortlessly. It was hilarious to play Frisbee with him during that time. I'd throw the disk and watch him take off like a bullet on his three good legs—the fourth one flapping and flopping in the air like a paper streamer caught in a huge gust of wind. I couldn't help but laugh uncontrollably at the sight of "Spaghetti Leg" tearing across the lawn. At times I thought that limp limb of his would flop forward and slap him in the face during one of his sprints! Trucker being Trucker, he took it all in stride and eventually had the last laugh. In time his leg strengthened and healed. He reached the point where one couldn't tell he had been operated on at all. The surgery gave him renewed mobility and a new lease on life. Sadly, he had to go through the procedure again in 2001. This time his right hip was done. Unfortunately his recovery was much different that time as he was nearing the end of his life and didn't have the same pep as before.

There was a ton of change in my family during the late nineties. In October of 1997, I purchased my first home and left Auburn Street for good. I had found a new house in Portland that was close to my work and ironically only three miles away from my parents. My brother got married in the spring of 1998 and moved out to Wyoming to pursue a career as a fire-fighter for the U.S. Forest Service. My family's sole remaining cat, Lucy, died of cancer (reminiscent of Sam) leaving just my mother, my father, and Trucker residing on Auburn Street. The nest had been thinned substantially, and certainly Trucker reaped most of the benefits. It's interesting to note that before Lucy died, she and Trucker had formed a noticeable bond unlike what you'd expect to see from a cat and dog. They seemed to look out for each other, and you got the feel that they could sense when something was wrong with either one of them. When Lucy was stricken with cancer she was noticeably sluggish and bloated. There were times I felt Trucker was looking out for her as best he could. It wasn't uncommon to see both of them share Trucker's bed together or eat from the same bowl. Lucy died in June of 1998, and my parents haven't had a cat since. She lived for fourteen years.

As the nineties waned, I saw less and less of Trucker. He and my mother were still an inseparable pair, but I really only saw him during visits to Auburn Street. I must say, I never noticed a dramatic or sudden decline in his physical health during his later years, but I do remember when he began to slow down. In time it was apparent he had lost some zip in his step, and he reached the point where he couldn't jump up into the car or navigate stairs without help, but for the most part, he got along quite well despite his age and previous injuries/surgeries. He remained remarkably active and mentally sharp even when his chin turned white.

In June of 2000, my father indulged a passion of his and bought a used 1988 Itasca motorhome. He was nearing retirement and had always yearned to tour the country. That same year, my brother and sister-in-law returned to Maine to put down permanent roots and start a family. They moved to Ellsworth so my brother could seek employment at nearby Acadia National Park. In July 2001, their first son Will was born. The young family moved again, this time to a larger house in Orland, not far from Ellsworth.

My parents—now promoted to grandparents—were anxious to spend time with their young grandson. Orland was a two-hour drive away from Portland, but with the motorhome, the trip was more enjoyable and convenient for all. Escorting my parents on their journeys to Orland was my maternal grandmother—a saint of a woman worthy of her own book—and of course Trucker. Although a bit aged, the motorhome was a great big bus that had all the necessities my parents desired. It had a stove, refrigerator, shower, toilet, bedroom, lots of storage space, and a little TV and VCR. All one really needed to do was stock it full of food, gas it up, and you were good to go for however long you desired to be on the road. What was even more convenient was that my brother's new residence had a long driveway with ample room to park the Itasca directly beside the house. From there, my father could hook into the power and enjoy a comfortable visit that didn't inconvenience or infringe upon anyone's space.

By the summer of 2001, Trucker was not his old self physically. He could still get around without much difficulty, but his ability to run, jump, and climb stairs unassisted had abandoned him. His face was noticeably grayer, and he was uncomfortable when needing to rise up from a sitting or lying position. Regardless of these apparent physical restrictions, his mind often betrayed his body and he constantly remained entrenched in his old habits, routines, and overall mischievous mindset. Despite his age, one still had to keep their eyes on Trucker or he'd find a way to fool you to get what he wanted or cause a little trouble.

In typical Trucker fashion, upon discovering the motorhome, he quickly staked out a claim, which happened to be in the front passenger seat! My grandmother was fascinated with the new vehicle and secretly desired to sit up front as well. Well, Trucker had determined that *he* wanted to sit up front and challenged (albeit playfully, I'm sure) my grandmother for that right. Not wanting to create friction with her canine friend (my grandmother was extremely fond of Trucker) she yielded her seat and allowed him the vaunted co-pilot's position. To make matters more interesting, the seat was fully reclined to allow Trucker to not only sit but lie on it during their travels. Comfort was of the utmost importance for him. I can just picture it now…the Itasca was like an earthbound *Millennium Falcon* cruising down the highway at much slower than light speed…and Trucker was Chewbacca to my father's Han Solo. What a sight to behold!

In mentioning my maternal grandmother—her name was Lena—I must remind everyone that she was very much a "cat person" and undoubtedly a catalyst for my mother herself becoming a cat person in her earlier years. But it's interesting to note that my grandmother, like my mother, changed. She liked and grew accustomed to Mandy in the early years and was enamored with Trucker much later on. She loved his foolishness and mischievous nature. She was greatly entertained by his tricks and would laugh non-stop whenever he got excited while opening presents. Though it may sound strange, I believe the two had a lot in common. My grandmother enjoyed life and loved having fun. She had an adventurous nature and didn't mind playfully upsetting the apple cart from time to time. Her advanced years didn't stop her from dressing up on Halloween—one of her favorite holidays—or playing a little joke on someone. She loved to write silly poems about friends or family members and was the master at creating and assigning foolish nick-names to all creatures—human or otherwise—that meant something to her. She loved traveling, parties, holidays, and family gatherings. She'd bring or even create games to play that usually meant prizes for the winners. Trucker was never excluded when there were prizes or presents to hand out.

My grandmother was never one to step back from a challenge either. One never told her what she was or was not capable of doing no matter how mentally or physically challenging it seemed. She had her own surprising mindset on such matters and would inevitably shock you by accomplishing something you claimed she *shouldn't*, or worse, *couldn't* do. She had an independent streak in her that complimented her other attributes. She did what she wanted to do in life, and she always seemed to have fun with it. I think Trucker, in his own way, did and acted very much the same. He did what he wanted to do and had fun doing it. He was silly and carefree in many ways, and those characteristics were showcased whenever he was dressed up in a hat and sunglasses—which happened often. Like my grandmother, he even took part in Halloween one year, when my mother dressed him up in a Batman costume designed for dogs. If he could speak, he wouldn't tell you he felt silly or foolish, he would ask for a ride in the Batmobile to the park where hopefully you had a Batarang to throw for him!

My grandmother was very remarkable in many ways, and she was very fond of Trucker. The two enjoyed each other's company and undoubtedly caused some mischief together, especially during the motorhome trips. But the most important similarity the two shared was this: My grandmother loved my mother and reveled in her happiness. Trucker was the same way… enough said.

By the summer of 2002, I accompanied my parents to a family gathering in Orland. They drove up with my grandmother and Trucker in the motorhome, and I took my car up separately. I did a lot of filming with my video camera during that trip, and I'm glad that I did. Little did I know that it would be the last time I ever captured Trucker on videotape. He was sluggish and in obvious discomfort at that time. He had slowed down tremendously, and even his eternally juvenile mind appeared to have succumbed to his failing body. Sadly the end was nearing; it was just a question of when and where.

I remember getting the call at home. It was my father who informed me that the end had come and that Trucker was put down at the vet's earlier in the day. It was September 2002. Like Mandy before him, Trucker's hindquarters had worn out and he lost the ability to stand. Immobile, and most assuredly in pain, he became unresponsive and unwilling to eat or drink anything. The time had come, and old Trucker simply lay down and waited to die. I remember meeting up with my father soon after. The actual elapsed time escapes me…it could have been a day or two later…but we sat and ate lunch at a nearby restaurant. He was visibly upset, with swollen eyes, trying to fight back the buildup of tears. He explained what had happened and how he and my mother were dealing with it. It was the first time in my life that I had seen my father so shaken up over the loss of a family pet. I shed many a tear myself in the days that followed.

My mother, of course, was hit the hardest. She tried to hide it in the presence of others, but it was more than obvious how devastated she was at the loss of her dog. Trucker had no stronger bond than that which had developed between him and my mother. Their lives and daily routines were so entwined that I'm sure my mother felt a great deal of confusion accompanying her overwhelming sadness. It was most assuredly hard for her to cope with the loss considering how close they had become. I didn't witness her grief on a daily basis, but when I did visit, it was obvious to me that she was in considerable anguish. I often wondered what would happen next.

Trucker lived from 1988 to 2002. He spent half his life in Alaska and the other half in Maine. He was mischievous, silly, naughty, very intelligent, and—most of all—loyal and lovable. He taught me a lot about himself and dogs in general. Up until I first met Trucker, all I knew was what I had learned from bringing up Mandy. Trucker taught me that not all dogs were uncontrollable and untrainable. He proved to me that dogs didn't need to be leashed or restrained one hundred percent of the time or else they'd just run off. Lastly he showed me a sense of loyalty and intelligence unlike anything I had ever seen in a dog. He really opened up my eyes to just how remarkable and special black Labs are, and I am very grateful for that. Though my time spent with Trucker was limited compared to Mandy (and the next canine you're about to be introduced too), I do think of him from time to time. Every once in a while he's brought up in family conversation, undoubtedly because of some foolish or naughty thing he did. His memory is preserved in pictures and video, and his ashes are kept alongside Mandy's on my parents' fireplace mantel. He had many endearing nicknames, including "T," "The T," and "Trucker T. Dog." Though born in the eighties and having lived into the early two thousands, Trucker will always be remembered as my mother's dog of the nineties. There is no doubt in my mind that "The T" has gone to that special place where all good animals go, still wearing that signature blue collar of his, and chasing down a Frisbee.

Memories

TRUCKER PHOTOGRAPHS

Trucker, posed for a formal picture.

Trucker just chilling in the "sunken" living room.

Trucker, making himself at home on Auburn Street circa 1994.

Trucker getting comfy on his L.L. Bean bed.

Trucker lying on a "black Lab" rug with a similar likeness.

Trucker getting ready to demonstrate his famous dog treat trick.

Trucker most likely celebrating his first birthday in Maine.

Trucker doing what he loved…opening presents.

Big or small, Trucker opened every wrapped present put in front of him.

Trucker had a style all his own. He was very unpredictable.

Trucker seemingly digging his way to China. Notice the huge tongue coated in dirt!

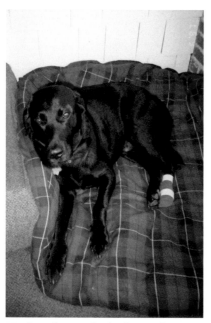

Trucker relaxing after his famous foot injury.   *Trucker showcasing his Alaskan roots with a big fur hat.*

Trucker sporting some Red Sox gear. Yours truly in the background.

Yours truly, my grandmother, and Trucker circa 2000.

CHAPTER THREE

DILLON

B y the late fall of 2002, my mother's despair over the death of Trucker had reached its zenith. She dearly missed having a dog and began actively searching for another one. My grandmother, who herself was extremely distraught over my mother's grief, strongly encouraged her to seek out a new canine companion immediately. She even offered to pay for the animal when the right one was found. My mother, discreetly at first, then more openly, took to the Internet and began searching for another cherished black Lab.

In relatively short time, she found exactly what she was looking for. A breeder located in Dover-Foxcroft, Maine, had a young, trained, male black Lab that was just the right age for acquisition. His name was Dillon, and he was originally being bred to be a show dog. Unfortunately, he had two bottom teeth that were misaligned, thus disqualifying him from being a serious contender. It's also interesting to note that Dillon was also wanted by the U.S. Border Patrol to assist in detecting and preventing undesirable elements and contraband from entering the United States via Mexico—an admirable, honorable, and very prestigious request, but one utterly and completely unsuitable for Dillon for reasons that will become quite apparent very shortly.

Like Trucker, Dillon was a male purebred black Lab. His coat was black all over and had a dark, lustrous sheen to it, and he was slightly smaller than Trucker in my estimation. Also, in contrast to Trucker, Dillon had a rounder head and a much shorter snout. His tail was in constant motion and would rapidly thump against the floor whenever he was happy or excited about something—which was most of the time. He too had a big pink tongue, but it wasn't as distinct as Trucker's in my opinion. One curious habit of Dillon's concerning his tongue was the frequent lip licking he would do.

He'd sit there with his mouth closed, and then suddenly the tip of his tongue would emerge just long enough to wet the upper and lower parts of his lips before retreating back into his mouth. He did this quite often. Normally one would often witness a dog open their mouths wide and broadly swipe their tongues back and forth until every inch of their jaw was slathered in saliva; not Dillon…his tongue shot out and shot back in like a snake's. It was certainly a peculiar thing to see.

Dillon arrived at Auburn Street on December 1, 2002. He was born on April 3, 2001, making him twenty months old when he became a Morin. He was a full-sized dog, fully housebroken, and had undergone previous obedience training. He was excited and bursting with energy the first time I met him—typical lab characteristics. He was fitted with a bright red collar so as not to inadvertently associate or bring up sad memories of Trucker.

Dillon would have his own signature color—red—as Trucker had blue before him. I believe my mother consciously tried to differentiate Dillon and Trucker. I think she didn't want to give anyone the impression that she was simply going to replace Trucker with another dog that would inevitably be just a younger clone. Dillon had his own distinguishing characteristics, his own personality, his own accoutrements, and his own life. He didn't simply come in and be expected to turn into another Trucker nor was he treated that way. He was his own distinct canine, and most assuredly my *mother's* new dog.

My mother wasn't crazy about the name Dillon, but she didn't change it because she felt the dog already knew and identified with it. It sparked some new and silly nicknames that he would be called throughout his life. Names such as "Dilly" and "Dill-Dog" were commonly used. I myself had an unflattering nickname that I called Dillon almost exclusively shortly after I first met him. It was a nickname that I felt summed up his personality utterly and completely. However, out of respect for my mother, who didn't care for it, I shall not mention it here. (I also had an unbecoming nickname for Trucker, which I also will not disclose out of respect.) One temporary nickname used in Dillon's youth was "Rocket Dog." He had a habit of easily getting excited and then racing up and down the hallway at full speed. It was a wonder he didn't stumble and crash through a wall!

Dillon was completely "humanized." He and my mother quickly became un-dividable and she took him everywhere she went. At home, he was given every comfort and courtesy my mother could provide (with some excep-tions of course). She spared no expense where he was concerned. He was given multiple luxurious beds to sleep on courtesy of L.L. Bean and Orvis, he was served only super premium dry dog food sold at specialty dog stores, he was showered in toys and other novelties that struck my mother's fancy, he was chauffeured in comfort (like Trucker before him) to various parks, trails, lakes, and beaches where he could run and frolic in the water, and his image was put on stamps and captured in pictures, drawings, and paintings hundreds upon hundreds of times. There were honestly more pictures taken of Dillon over a span of thirteen years than taken of me over my entire life!

To say that Dillon was spoiled was an understatement, but nobody cared or saw it as offensive, as my mother was not one to broadcast it or ex-pound on her dog's greatness to others. She was humble concerning Dillon, and, curiously, the dog didn't act in any sort of pretentious manner. The way he did act was funny and quirky in its own right.

Dillon had a curious, if not childishly peculiar, personality that changed very little throughout his life. First and foremost, he was the most lovable dog a person could meet. All it took was one simple pat on the head and you were hooked. He would love you forever after that and remain at your side until your hand cramped up from repeated petting. He would cuddle up close to you and lovingly put his head in your lap while looking up at you with big puppy-dog eyes that would melt your heart.

Dillon didn't dislike anyone from my estimation. He cheerfully and enthusiastically greeted a stranger just as he would someone he knew, but he barely barked at anyone or anything. He was undoubtedly the quietest dog I have ever known. He didn't whimper, whine, or ever bark uncontrollably. There were times I wondered if he even had vocal cords! From a personal-ity standpoint, he didn't have Mandy's wild side or Trucker's penchant for causing mischief. He didn't ever try to run off or regularly tangle with native wildlife. He loved the company of other dogs but was perfectly content with just being around my mother.

To sum it all up accurately and honestly, Dillon was a big baby. No one who knew him well could ever dispute that. Bravery was not at the forefront of his list of personality traits. He was afraid of his own shadow, and at times extremely timid. He was not a fan of stairs, and in the beginning he refused to go up and down them. He would fidget and whimper until someone stood by his side and traversed the steps with him. He would get down real low and practically crawl on his belly when going up and down. Over time, he eventually gained enough courage to do it himself, but I don't think he was ever one hundred percent comfortable with staircases.

What was even more peculiar was his phobia with strange or unfamiliar surfaces. He literally was afraid of crossing floors he was unacquainted with. A good example was the kitchen floor in my house. Every time Dillon was brought over for a visit, he hesitated and wouldn't cross the linoleum unless forced to by my mother. He was like a little child afraid to cross a busy street or step into a swimming pool for the first time. Once he got over the floor and onto the living room carpet, he was fine, but that's where he'd stay until forced to cross the dreaded kitchen linoleum again to exit the house. And it was not just my floor, or even exclusively indoor surfaces that rattled him. He was just as spooked by the outdoors. To the casual observer, he was fine on grass, dirt, and pavement; but to the trained eye, one could easily detect patterns in his choice of travel routes. He would choose the same and often indirect path to and from places. He would zigzag and often go completely around large swaths of empty, harmless ground to get where he was going. It was comical to watch and quite odd. Inside the house on Auburn Street, he would quite frequently step from area rug to area rug to avoid the ceramic tiled kitchen floor or the hardwood floors in the dining room. We likened him to a bullfrog jumping from lily pad to lily pad on a placid pond. Generally he was fine with any carpeted area unless the carpets quickly changed color from room to room as is often the case. In that instance, there could be problems. His behavior caused us to dub him as being a little neurotic, and that psychological term stuck with him for the duration of his life.

Initially, Dillon was uncomfortable riding in cars. I would guess that it was because he had little experience in cars during his very young life. And when he did ride in vehicles prior to my mother's SUV, he was always crated. Well, my mother had no interest in taking him anywhere in a crate—or having him crated for any reason—so he quickly had to adapt to riding along with her. In time he got used to it and toward the end of his life, felt most comfortable in the back of her car. But unlike Trucker, Dillon had no interest in riding shotgun and kept to the back where a nice blanket and comfy bed were always present.

Dillon was extraordinarily clingy, especially where my mother was concerned. He never wanted to be alone under any circumstances, but he absolutely dreaded being away from my mother. As I mentioned previously, the two were inseparable, and Dillon would follow my mother everywhere she went throughout the house—and I do mean everywhere. He particularly liked to linger directly behind her whenever she was in the kitchen preparing food. My father certainly had his own time with Dillon, and the two of them went off for their own walks and exercise sessions, but the dog was never away from my mother for any extended length of time if it could be helped. He was noticeably sadder whenever apart from the person he adored the most. I picked up on that the few times I walked him alone. Sometimes his obsessive clinginess was annoying, and you'd just have to tell him to, "Go lie down!" He was unquestionably a big baby.

I think I can honestly say that, after my mother, I was Dillon's favorite person. I would visit Auburn Street frequently and always be greeted first by that silly dog. In his youth he would race up to me and practically jump in my arms. If I ever sat on the floor, he would instantly come over and nuzzle me with his wet nose or lie with his head in my lap. He was very affectionate and quickly discovered that I was the person most likely to sit and pat him the longest.

Dillon was my pal, and I loved to play with him and tease him. He had no interest in Frisbees, like Trucker did. Instead he preferred a toy called an Air Dog, which was a long cylindrical object with a short knotted rope sticking out of one end. Essentially it looked like someone had elongated a tennis ball and attached a rope to it. Well, Dillon loved it. One of his favorite games was to have someone (like me) throw the Air Dog off the back deck and into the back yard. He would chase after it with reckless abandon but not extreme intelligence. Sometimes it would be right in front of him and he couldn't find it until you pointed it out! His nose, like any dog's, was constantly sniffing out scents whenever he was outside, but Dillon hardly had the nose of a bloodhound. Sometimes I wondered if it worked at all, as his ability to find things was sorely lacking—in my opinion. Eventually he'd return with the Air Dog, and then the real fun would begin. He never wanted to relinquish it. Instead he always wanted me to engage in a tug-of-war with him, where he'd surprise you with a low growl as if trying to act tough. Most of the time you couldn't get the Air Dog away from him. I would eventually give up and ignore him. Sometimes that'd work, he'd drop the toy, and we'd resume play. Other times it didn't, and he'd just hang onto it until he got bored and wanted to go back inside.

It was my father who figured out the key to winning the tug-of-war game with Dillon. He'd throw the Air Dog and wait for Dillon to come back with it. When he arrived and tried to initiate the tug-of-war, my father would simply grab the rope and not pull on it. He'd hold it limply and tell Dillon to drop it. After a few seconds, Dillon would release it without any hassle. My father would reward him by throwing it again. Sometimes I'd get creative with the Air Dog and take it into the front yard. Dillon would watch me as I would heave it clear over the house and into the back yard. He'd then race around the side of the house and try to find where it landed. I used to time how long it took for him to locate the toy. Sometimes he found it right away; other times it took him a while! Regardless, we always had fun.

Like Mandy and Trucker before him, Dillon quickly realized that his best bet for table scraps was to hang out by me during meals—which he did faithfully. Only now it was much harder. My mother didn't allow Dillon to be fed from the table and often scolded anyone who was caught doing so. She restricted his diet to his own special dog food and occasional dog treats. She didn't like him eating scraps from the table—a big departure from Mandy, who got bones directly from the table, and Trucker, who was fattened up nicely from human food.

I certainly was no longer a regular at my parents' dinner table, as I didn't live on Auburn Street anymore, but I did find myself dining there from time to time. And yes, my pal did help me dispose of some unwanted food when my mother wasn't looking. (Fortunately, Hamburger Pie was never served to me in those years!) It's worth noting that Dillon did get a variety of treats, however. He was served several types of specialty dog bones and jerky. Occasionally a dog biscuit would end up on the tip of his nose, and he'd do the flip and catch trick just like Trucker had before him. But the one unfailing staple he received after dinner every night was a frozen treat called Frosty Paws. It was an ice cream cup formulated for dogs, and Dillon loved them. I can't imagine the amount of money my mother spent consistently buying box after box of the canine treats over the years, but Dillon rarely went without.

Dillon was lovable and funny in other ways. I'd sit on my parents' couch and he'd climb up next to me and then roll over on his back and sit there like a person would. He'd then rest his head on my shoulder. My maternal grandmother witnessed this act one day and couldn't contain her laughter. She also loved it when Dillon would roll on his back and nap with his legs stuck up in the air. Sadly, I must note that my grandmother was acquainted with Dillon for only a very short time as she fell ill in late 2003. She was taken into the hospital in the spring of 2004, where she was diagnosed with pancreatic cancer. She would eventually succumb to the illness in June of 2004. She was eighty-nine years old and would have easily made it to one hundred in my opinion if not stricken with cancer. Even though she didn't know Dillon for nearly as long as she knew Mandy and Trucker, she definitely witnessed the initial joy and happiness he brought to my mother, and that alone was worth its weight in gold in her eyes—I'm sure of that.

One other sad note worth mentioning is that the motorhome trips up to Orland ceased when my grandmother passed. With Trucker's death in 2002 and my grandmother's departure in 2004, the joy of the motorhome was no longer evident or appreciated. My parents were able to salvage one or two trips up to Orland in the summer of 2003, but I don't think things were the same. My grandmother undoubtedly was not physically herself in those days, and Dillon surely didn't take to the motorhome like Trucker did.

With those two key elements missing, there wasn't enough interest to keep the old Itasca in service. With little use from 2003 to 2004, the motorhome was eventually sold in 2005.

A really important part of Dillon's life that my parents keyed on was his exercise. He was a young and very energetic dog when he first came into their lives, and I know they didn't want to stifle his drive and vigor. My mother, in wanting to grant him more freedom than either Mandy or Trucker ever had, and in staying vigilant in protecting him from the ever-present dangers of the Auburn Street traffic, invested in an underground electric dog fence that would ring the perimeter of the Morin property. The fence was installed and Dillon was fitted with a special collar that would gently shock him whenever he got too close to the fence. In theory the whole setup was great. Dillon could be let out of the house anytime and allowed to roam both the back and front yards at his leisure, without supervision, and with no danger of being struck by a vehicle. On paper it was a great idea, but in practice it was a total flop—but not for the reasons you may suspect.

Dillon never, in my recollection, expressed a desire to bolt. He simply never wanted to run off like Mandy and Trucker did. He was perfectly content to stay put and was happiest when no more than two feet away from my mother. He also learned quickly where the fence perimeter was, and, after the initial shock, never tested the boundary line again. Collar or no collar, there were obvious limits to where he would go. The most obvious was in the front driveway. He would not pass a certain point even though it was well inside the fence perimeter. In short, it became apparent that Dillon was a very low risk for running into the street and getting hit by a car. The fence, in my opinion, was unnecessary and unneeded. My parents kept it, however, and faithfully strapped on his shock collar when let outside in the yard. My mother feared some animal might appear and entice a chase that would lead Dillon into the road and imminent danger. Strangely enough, I believe the person that received the most shocks was my father and not the dog! Occasionally he'd slip the collar in his pocket and forget it was there until he got zapped after crossing the fence perimeter!

My parents experimented with lots of places to take Dillon for daily exercise. In his early days, my mother would take him to Willard Beach in Cape Elizabeth. She has often described to me his unbridled excitement upon arrival. He loved the beach and running in the sand. He got the chance to mingle with other dogs and take a dip in the ocean. It was definitely one of his most favorite places to go. Unfortunately it was not the most convenient location. It took some time to get there and was often crowded. My parents continued to explore closer options.

Another favorite locale was the nearby Highland Lake. It was not a terribly far drive, and it had a nice little boat launch area where Dillon could easily jump into the water and retrieve the thrown Air Dog. My parents took him up there a lot, as he loved the water. Out of all three dogs, I think Dillon liked the water the most. Mandy was known to jump into lakes and the ocean, but she wasn't a great swimmer and rarely ever had the opportunity unfortunately. Trucker had the opportunity but wasn't really interested in bodies of water. He'd get wet, but one could tell that it really wasn't his cup of tea. Dillon, on the other hand, took to water like a fish or a duck. He loved to swim and retrieve up at Highland Lake. Trips up there became regular occurrences, and there are lots of funny pictures of him bounding into the water.

One story that cannot go without mention concerning Highland Lake involved a funny incident that happened to my mother. She and Dillon went up there one day on a routine exercise excursion. Dillon jumped into the water as he always did and went out a little farther than my mother was comfortable with. Fearing her dog might drown, my mother went to the water's edge and frantically called for Dillon to come back. Unbeknownst to her, my mother had entered a marshy area laden with mud. Distracted by the dog who was doing his best impression of a channel swimmer, and most likely heading for the middle of the lake, my mother began to gradually sink into the muck. Before she realized what was happening, she was knee deep in mud and still sinking. Eventually she quickly found herself waist deep and unable to free herself! As she struggled to get loose, Dillon calmly swam back to shore. Unfortunately, Dillon was hardly Lassie and couldn't help my mother escape her little quicksand trap, nor did he rush off to get help.

He most likely just stood there foolishly looking dumb while my mother continued to sink.

Fortunately the story has a happy ending, though. As luck would have it, there was a nearby kayaker who was able to lend a hand. Using a paddle, the kayaker was able to pull my mother out of the mud and onto solid ground. I'm sure she was deeply embarrassed and lost a shoe or two that day, but, knowing my mother like I do, her main concern and relief was that Dillon didn't inadvertently drown himself in the lake. I imagine it was a very uncomfortable ride home that day. It probably took a while to remove all the mud and wet dog smell from the car after that little episode!

Highland Lake was certainly a Dillon destination, but there was one place that truly became his official arena of daily dog exercise. My father had experimented with taking him on hikes on local parts of the Portland trail system. One day he happened to be in Falmouth and he discovered the Falmouth Community Park that was conveniently just a few minutes drive from their house. The place was ideal for dogs, as there was lots of open space for them to run and explore. Dillon was taken there regularly at all times of the day and all seasons of the year.

It was at the Falmouth Community Park where Dillon and my mother met and formed a special friendship with another Lab lover. Her name was Pam Dixon, and she was in possession of two Labs—a yellow and a chocolate. Their names were Murphy and Bandit. Dillon, Murphy, and Bandit become fast friends and loved to play together at the park. They formed their own little group, which Pam and my mother affectionately named "The Lab Gang." I would occasionally hear stories about Pam Dixon and "The Lab Gang" during visits to my parents' house. In time, the Falmouth Community Park was nicknamed the "Dog Park" by my folks. I took it a step further and playfully nicknamed Pam "Dog Park Dixon." Little did I know that my mother shared my nickname with her, and the first time I met her face to face at one of my book signings, she happily shook my hand and introduced herself as "Dog Park Dixon."

There were a lot of good memories shared between my mother, Pam, and their dogs at the "Dog Park." Unfortunately, as I write this, all three dogs are now deceased. Bandit passed in 2012, with Murphy being the last to peacefully expire in 2015. However, my mother and Pam are still good friends who see each other often and continue to share their love of Labs. It's amazing how animals can bring people together and forge new friendships. It's even more amazing how dogs—particularly Labs—are especially good at it.

In 2003, the house on Auburn Street underwent a major interior renovation. My parents decided that the entire living space on the first floor needed to be upgraded. That included a brand new kitchen, dining room, living room, master bathroom and master bedroom, as well as the creation of a new exterior deck off the old "sunken" living room. All the major appliances were replaced with new ones, the countertops were all torn out and redesigned, the flooring was replaced, several walls were removed, a new staircase was constructed, new lighting fixtures and plumbing were installed, the ceilings were redone, and the walls were all repainted after extensive electrical rewiring was complete. It was a monumental undertaking that required several months to finish and caused much disruption and discomfort for my parents. While all this work was being done, they were driven upstairs and into my brother's old bedroom to sleep. My old bedroom, although larger, was unavailable, as it had been previously transformed into a new children's bedroom/playroom to accommodate my nephew Will, who was two years old at the time. Fortunately, as mentioned earlier, there was a full bathroom that connected the two bedrooms.

The basement of the house was transformed into the new temporary kitchen. A secondary refrigerator was already located down there and was soon joined by a well-used microwave oven and stove. All meals had to be prepared with limited means in an inconvenient setting. Fortunately there was a big laundry room sink located downstairs that allowed for washing up. There was also a TV for viewing. I can imagine my parents' extreme irritation during the whole process.

The garage and basement became the primary storage areas for all the displaced furniture and personal possessions that had to be moved while the renovation was taking place. It must have taken seemingly endless hours to properly box up and move an entire floor's worth of belongings. I give my parents credit. It was a huge burden to assume physically, emotionally, and of course financially. The project started just after Labor Day of 2003 and was finished the week before Thanksgiving of that same year. My mother was worried it would not be complete before the holidays. Fortunately, most everything was in place and somewhat back to normal by the time we sliced into our Thanksgiving Day turkey.

The house looked great when it was complete. Some new furniture was brought in to compliment the new dining room, living room, bedroom, and kitchen. The kitchen was completely redesigned and enlarged. The linoleum and carpet were torn up and replaced with ceramic tile, and the countertops were now granite. The hot tub, shower, and sink in the new master bathroom were highlighted with decorative marble, and nice hardwood flooring was installed in the new dining room. A new guest bathroom was installed, and a walk-in closet was created alongside a new laundry area adjacent and inter-connected to the master bedroom. This allowed my parents more privacy and easier access to the bathroom, their clothes, and the new washer and dryer now conveniently located by the bedroom and not down in the basement. There were small problems that arose shortly after completion, and it took awhile for everything and everyone to settle in and get used to the changes, but overall it was a tremendous improvement and well worth the effort.

Dillon, I'm told, took everything in stride. I was convinced that his neurotic nature and quirkiness with change would make him very uneasy and unhappy with what was happening all around him. However, that was not the case. I'm told he acted quite normally and was simply curious about all the changes being implemented. In fact, he was probably less stressed than my parents. Even without defined lily pads to jump back and forth onto, he maneuvered quite well through the rubble-strewn chaos that was my parents' primary living space. He picked up the daily routine without much hassle. Upstairs meant bedtime; downstairs meant meals and TV. In all, I don't think he minded the renovation, nor do I think it bothered him.

Not only did the interior of the house on Auburn Street dramatically change over the years, but the exterior did too. The prized swimming pool with the inflatable dome was one of the first unavoidable major failures the aging house experienced. Long before the 2003 interior renovation, the pool began to fall into serious disrepair. The pool liner leaked, and the dome (which was replaced entirely by a second one two or three years after we moved in) was slowly rotting away from increased amounts of mildew. In time, the pool pump failed and the furnace broke down. My father deemed that the cost of repairing everything was not in the family budget, and the pool sat unused and neglected for years. What's interesting to note is that the pool became unusable in the early nineties when Mandy was still alive and the final transformation of the back yard was not complete until the later years of Dillon's life.

Over a stretch of twenty-three years, the pool was drained, the inflatable dome discarded, the cabana bulldozed into the pool, the concrete deck torn up, the stone fireplace dismantled and hauled away, several trees cut down, and Mandy's old doghouse removed and destroyed. What remains today is a large, expansive back yard that for years served only as a place for the dogs to run and use as their personal toilets. Though I'm sure my father is glad his back yard is now much more open and spacious, I doubt he's happy about all the extra lawn mowing and fall leaf disposal he now has to endure! One final thing to mention about Auburn Street is that it has also undergone vinyl siding, new window, and new roof replacements. In October of 2016, my parents will have lived there for thirty-one years.

The Morin family grew during Dillon's tenure. In July of 2001, my oldest nephew, Will, was born. Interestingly enough, his first exposure to a family dog was Trucker. There are pictures of both him and Trucker together on the floor of my parents' living room. Although they did meet and share some time together, Will was far too young to remember Trucker, who died only a few months after his second birthday. Dillon, however, left a long and lasting impression on Will, and the two of them shared an extensive and rewarding relationship that I'm sure my nephew will remember for the rest of his life.

"Will and Dill" grew up together in a similar way to how Mandy and I did. Will was fascinated with Dillon from a very young age, and it didn't take long for the two to become friends. As a toddler, Will would climb all over Dillon and try to hug and snuggle with him. Oftentimes he'd lie down next to him on the floor and pretend to go to sleep with him. During many visits to "Grandma's house," which is what Will always called my parents' residence, Will liked to make little forts from couch cushions or from blankets draped over pieces of furniture or countertops. After doing so, he often tried to get Dillon to crawl inside them with him. Sometimes he'd just cover Dillon with a blanket and pretend to tuck him in wherever it was he happened to be lying at the time. Dillon took it all in stride and tolerated the peculiar little human that occasionally visited. Dillon didn't have much or possibly *any* experience being around children before Will popped into his life. Dillon tolerated Will's little antics the best he could and he was always very calm and patient with the child. Once in a while he'd reach the point where he'd had enough and would scamper off—usually to seek protection and comfort from my mother.

When Will grew a little older, he loved to take Dillon outside and throw the *Air Dog* for him. In the beginning it was very funny to watch, as Will wasn't able to throw the toy very far and Dillon didn't know whether to retrieve it or simply let it lie where it landed—sometimes only a foot or two from where Will stood! In time, as Will got bigger, he was able to throw the Air Dog greater distances and watch Dillon chase after it. Will loved to rummage around in Dillon's toy chest and he would always appear with random chew toys to present to the dog in hopes he might put on a little show either by chewing or chasing something. A young dog is the perfect compliment for a toddler as both have seemingly endless amounts of energy to expend on each other for both exercise and entertainment.

We had to keep our eyes on Will where Dillon was concerned. Will was always fascinated with balls, bats, and anything that could launch a projectile of sorts. (It's a fascination that has stuck with him even to this day.) He especially loved water guns, Nerf guns, and bow and arrow sets. He was right in heaven whenever given the opportunity to shoot something at someone—human or otherwise. Unfortunately, Dillon was often targeted. Will *never* went after him in a violent or malicious manner—it was never his intention to hurt the dog—but some of the shooting toys he had could have injured Dillon if they struck him in the right area. With that in mind, we always had to make sure Will was watched whenever "wielding a toy weapon" in the dog's presence. Fortunately there were never any accidents, and neither Will nor Dill were harmed when playing together. In time, when Will was old enough to understand, we were able to teach him that he should never throw or shoot anything at Dillon. I think Dillon was grateful for that lesson!

Another thing that fascinated Will concerning Dillon was "treats and tricks." Will always begged "Grandma" to have permission to feed Dillon a treat in hopes that he would do an entertaining trick for him too. He'd take him through the usual commands, always including "sit" and "lie down," but far and away his favorite was the "flip and catch the treat off the nose" trick. When Will was young he could have watched Dillon do that trick for an hour and not gotten tired of it. Dillon would have hung in there for that long too—provided the treats kept coming!

Dillon was very obedient and mindful. His occasional neurotic behavior often gave people the impression that he wasn't very intelligent, but to be totally fair, Dillon was not brainless. I would tease him incessantly about being a "dummy," but in reality he was more of a coddled and timorous "baby" than anything else. To entertain Will (and myself), I would rapidly but gently drum on the top of Dillon's head with one hand. The sound echoing through his closed mouth resembled something similar to what one would hear while tapping on a hollow bamboo log! I used to tell Will that Dillon had a hollow head.

Dillon was not wild and mindlessly destructive like Mandy, nor was he independently adventurous and cunning like Trucker. Dillon was the meekest and most lovable of the three in my opinion. He didn't seek out danger and adventure, nor did he ever destroy the house or want to run free. Dillon was happiest in a serene setting, close to my mother, while either being patted or fed. He did like to run and play with other dogs in open spaces outdoors, but he never desired to be out of eye or earshot of any family member ever. This was a very convenient personality trait for Dillon to possess, as it kept him out of a lot danger. I often think back to whoever made the call from the U.S. Border Patrol requesting Dillon be trained to track drug smugglers and illegal immigrants. Boy did they dodge a bullet. A newborn baby kitten would have been a braver, more suitable, and more qualified applicant for that job than Dillon!

In June of 2008, my second nephew Jack was born. (Actually, he was named John, but everyone in the family calls him Jack—except when he's in trouble…then it's John.) Dillon was seven years old when he was first introduced to my buddy, "Wolfman Jack." Naturally a few years went by before the two fully interacted with each other, but Jack's interest in Dillon differed from Will's. Jack wasn't as fascinated with Dillon as Will was. He didn't ignore him, but he didn't seek him out either. He loved to watch Will make Dillon do tricks, and be silly in general, but the cuddling and outward displays of affection weren't nearly as evident from Jack as they had been from Will at his age.

There certainly wasn't anything wrong with Jack's attitude toward Dillon; it was just different from his brother's, as most siblings tend to be. Jack simply had other interests that kept him occupied and entertained. One must also note that Dillon was no longer a young and energetic dog when Jack became old enough to really interact and appreciate him. This small fact could possibly explain why Jack was not as engaged with him as Will was in years prior. Nevertheless, both boys loved Dillon and showed him affection in their own personal ways. There are countless photos and video shot of Dillon and the boys over the course of his life. The two grandchildren and Dillon became the most important parts of my mother's existence and she seized on every opportunity to spend time with them together.

I myself had a special bond with Dillon. I knew him longer and saw him much more frequently than Trucker. I used to watch him whenever my parents went somewhere that wasn't suitable for dogs. My mother despised leaving him alone under any circumstances and would reach out to anyone who could step up and keep him company. He had a few "babysitters," including Burke Waldron's father, but the duty regularly fell in my lap, and I never minded spending time with my pal. Dillon would sulk and pout anytime he was separated from my mother, no matter the duration. My job was to cheer him up and get his mind on other things. I'd wrestle with him on the floor, let him up on the furniture so he could lie in my lap, pump him full of Frosty Paws, and pat him endlessly. I'd also order takeout and feed him from the table without any fear of reprisals from my mother. (Later in his life I curbed this habit as his vet had discovered that Dillon was allergic to most meats. He would suffer from constant ear infections, which the vet diagnosed was the result of an allergic reaction. My mother would give him prescribed eardrops that made him rub his head on the carpet and make him look like he was having a seizure. It was very funny to watch.) Dillon and I would watch TV together and fool around in the yard until my parents got home. You never saw a happier dog in your entire life than when Dillon saw my mother reenter the house.

In Dillon's later years he and I played a game together that I dubbed "Driveway Food," which I will explain. I was (and still am for that matter) invited to Auburn Street once a week in the evenings for Sunday dinner. When the weather was agreeable, I was often placed in charge of the grill to cook up whatever meat was being served for dinner. The grill was brought out from the garage into the driveway. Dillon often kept me company as I cooked. I like to think that he was just happy to see me and enjoyed hanging out, but I'm sure the real reason was because there was hot meat on the grill and he knew his best chance of getting some was from me. My mother stored Dillon's dry dog food in the garage. She'd scoop out the exact amount he was to be fed and dump it in his dish. Within two seconds, the entire contents of the bowl were inhaled. Dillon was a real "chow hound" and would devour food in record time. I don't believe he knew how to chew. Most of the time he would just "inhale" food and swallow it down whole. As docile and lovable as Dillon was, one had to be careful when feeding him by hand. He would aggressively chomp at your fingers to get the goodies they held. Many a time his fangs came down hard on my fingertips, causing appreciable pain and an occasional cut!

To get Dillon out of my way while I grilled, and to provide me with a little entertainment, I devised Driveway Food. Knowing he had already eaten and also knowing that my mother would disapprove, I would sneak a few handfuls of his dry dog food and toss them high into the air. The food would land and scatter all over the driveway. Dillon, thinking it was raining chow from heaven, would rush into the driveway and scarf down the food pellet by pellet. His nose would go into overdrive and he'd scurry from spot to spot after locking in on a tasty morsel. He wouldn't stop searching until he was satisfied he had gotten every last scrid. Sometimes he needed a little help locating the last remnants, but in the end he would always get it all. It was comical to watch and it kept him from bugging me while I cooked.

Even though I playfully denied it at first, it didn't take long for my mother to figure out what I was doing and scold me for it. However, that made it all the more fun and I continued to do it. Dillon of course loved it and anxiously waited for me to toss the food every time I grilled. It got to the point where he'd jump up and down and whine next to the bag of dog food until I grabbed a handful. Like a sprinter lining up on the blocks and waiting for the starting gun to fire, Dillon would faithfully line up on the edge of the driveway and watch me intently just before the food was catapulted into the air. At that point he would rush out and do his thing. We had fun with our little game and it soon got to the point where my mother enjoyed doing it too. There were a few drawbacks, however. Unfortunately Dillon got a little too used to it and expected us to play every time I came over and was even remotely close to the garage food bag. During the very few times my mother absolutely forbade me to feed him, he would still stand by the edge of the driveway and wait for me throw the handfuls into the air. There were even times when he was forced to come inside the house because he wouldn't leave the driveway until we played our game. Lastly and most sadly, as he aged, his legs grew weaker and his midsection would sag. Many times he would stumble or smack his jaw hard against the pavement when going after the food. Eventually I had to just stop playing the game with him, as I was just too afraid he would hurt himself. Nevertheless those good memories of the fun we had will stay with me forever.

Winter was a fun time for Dillon too. In his youth he would plow through layers of freshly fallen snow and roll around in it until his black coat turned white. Sometimes the Air Dog would get buried, and he wouldn't be able to find it until the snow melted away in the spring. Though he loved being outside in the cold, he equally adored being inside when a cozy fire was burning in the fireplace. Dillon and I shared a passion for fire. I loved to make them and watch them burn and he loved to lie in front of them and absorb the warmth. A good hearty blaze or a slow burning smolder just seems to hypnotize me and melt the stress away from my body and soul. Rarely do I ever pass up an opportunity to build a fire when visiting my folks on a cold winter evening.

Dillon loved to snuggle in front of the fire. Sometimes I'd either sit or lie on the floor directly in front of it. Without fail, Dillon would cuddle up next to me or lie on top of me outright. He could sit there for hours and be perfectly content, especially if someone was patting him. Many times he'd lie next to my mother's chair close to the fire and stay there without moving a muscle while she rocked and stroked his head. Occasionally if you weren't paying attention, you'd be surprised with a wet nose nuzzle or a sloppy lick.

Dillon was a creature of habit and routine, as was my mother. For years, the two of them would start their day early, with my mother attending her exercise class at Curves and Dillon patiently waiting in the car. They would then do errands together and inevitably end up at the "Dog Park" for additional exercise and playtime. In the afternoons my mother would work at her computer with Dillon comfortably laying on one of his many plush beds at her side. In the evenings, Dillon had a strict dinnertime and bathroom routine. He always ate at the same time and was let outside to relieve himself just before bed. My mother would employ a clever trick to get him to go out and pee, as he was often reluctant to do so. She would stand on the back deck and randomly toss dog biscuits into the yard. It was similar to the "Driveway Food" game and it encouraged him to hunt down the treats in the dark. It gave him a little last minute exercise and the chance for a private squirt before coming back in. It usually worked without fail and would spare my mother from having to get up earlier than normal to let him out with a full bladder.

My mother and Dillon were quite the pair. Wherever she went, he went. As the years gradually slid by, Dillon grew older and naturally began to slow down. As this happened, it became increasingly harder for my mother to keep up the daily routine. Soon Dillon couldn't hop up into the car without a little boost. Over time, the little boost turned into a big boost. Eventually he reached the point where he needed to be picked up entirely and lifted into the car. It's a cruel fate for Labs, and Dillon, like both Trucker and Mandy before him, was also a victim of slowly degenerating hindquarters.

As his body physically weakened, he wasn't able to do the things he loved with the same vitality he once had. Swimming at Highland Lake became rarer and rarer, and the trips to the "Dog Park" became shorter and shorter. As he grew older, some of his bad habits became more apparent. At some point in his life he began consuming any animal waste he could sniff out. When he got older it really became apparent. The medical term for it is "coprophagia," and Dillon suffered from it quite noticeably. He had to be watched fervently and cleaned up after immediately when outside as he didn't even discount his own feces. One other unpleasant physical feature Dillon had as he aged was an increasing amount of warts of the top of his head and other parts of his body. They were harmless, just unsightly. As he continued to age, the white hairs appeared around his chin and eyes in ever increasing numbers. Despite his physical aging, his mind stayed youthful and he still yearned to do the things he loved—always.

It's never pleasant to write about the decline and eventual passing of a beloved pet, but for the third time in this book, I must venture into those stormy seas and recall unpleasant memories I wish were not there. Dillon's decline was gradual. As the first decade of the two thousands came to a close, Dillon had slowed down considerably but was far from unable to function independently. He needed a little extra help from time to time with certain things, like getting in and out of the car, but was able to get around without too much difficulty. He reached the point where his normal running speed slowed down to a trot and his walking pace was reduced to a sluggish shuffle. His joints most assuredly began to bother him as he moved about, and my mother started giving him daily prescribed supplements and special vitamin enriched treats to ease any pain he could have been experiencing. Occasionally one of his legs would go lame and he was forced to rest—a very difficult task for any Lab.

Like his two predecessors before him, Dillon's world began to shrink as he grew older. Slick floors were always a danger and skillfully avoided whenever possible, and he generally began to steer clear of any interior surface that wasn't carpeted. Also, he was more willing to stay on grassy areas outside rather than maneuver on smooth pavement. In time, stairs became next to impossible for Dillon, and he eventually reached the point where he completely stopped trying to negotiate them—even if it meant being temporarily separated from my mother. He could handle a step or two, but a full set of stairs was out of the question.

The first major blow to Dillon's health occurred in June 2013. The weather was extremely hot, and he started to have wheezing/choking fits. To listen to him, you'd think he was simply trying to puke up some undesirable thing he ingested, but the problem was much deeper. When my mother first noticed it, she made sure to keep him relaxed and always in an air-conditioned environment. In the beginning, that seemed to work—at least temporarily. Gradually the problem worsened, and my mother, not wanting to take any chances, took Dillon to the vet. He was diagnosed with laryngeal paralysis, a degenerative nerve disorder affecting the muscles of the larynx, sedated, and kept overnight for observation. My mother arrived to take him home the next day. Unfortunately, upon returning home, his loud, raspy, breathing resumed in full force, and she insisted he remain at the vet's until the problem was properly diagnosed and a permanent treatment solution rendered.

On June 26th—my mother's birthday—Dillon underwent arytenoid lateralization surgery. Basically the cartilage and muscles around Dillon's larynx had become paralyzed and were closing off his windpipe, making it extremely difficult for him to breathe. It's a very common affliction for older large-breed dogs. The surgery to correct the problem required the blocking cartilage and paralyzed muscles to be "tied back" permanently, thus allowing more oxygen to flow freely into the lungs. Fortunately, the surgery was successful, and after some minor recovery time, Dillon was cleared to go home.

I remember that first day back as I was visiting and wanting to see how Dillon was doing. He was trembling a little and clearly expressing signs of distress, particularly whenever my mother ventured out of his sight. My mother tried to work in the kitchen preparing that evening's meal while my father sat in his usual chair in the nearby sunken living room watching the news on TV and reading the paper. I sat on the floor in front of the couch with Dillon's head in my lap. I petted him and tried to keep him calm, as that was critical for the healing process. Strangely, he barely responded to my actions and constantly craned his neck and head looking in the direction of where he thought my mother was. Several times he feebly tried to get up and walk into the kitchen, but I stopped him. All that evening he would only calm down whenever my mother was in sight or very near to him. It was the clearest and most defined example I had ever witnessed that showcased their close relationship and need for one another.

In time, Dillon fully recovered and no longer suffered from respiratory problems. The surgery effected the end of his time in the water, as the risk of drowning was too great. Though his breathing difficulties had subsided, the degeneration of his hindquarters did not. Unfortunately that problem was accelerated—a common but cruel side effect to the arytenoid lateralization surgery. Dillon was already behind the eight ball in that department as he had previously been diagnosed with hip dysplasia at the age of two. Now the problem was magnified, and it wasn't long before his struggles with it became apparent.

As 2013 gave way to 2014, Dillon's world shrank even further and he began having difficulty getting up and even more issues with walking. (His running days had abandoned him for good at that point.) He started to become incontinent and would occasionally have accidents in the house. His hindquarters became noticeably atrophied, and by the summer of that year, my parents had to fit him with a special thoracic harness to aid him in getting up and moving about. The condition only worsened and put a tremendous strain on my parents, as Dillon needed almost one hundred percent care and attention. He was never left alone under any circumstances in those days. My mother put the priority of her dog before anything else and sacrificed what little free time she had to tend to his needs unfailingly.

As an anniversary present that summer, I presented my parents with two tickets to a Willie Nelson concert in New Hampshire. The show didn't require an overnight stay, but it did mean that my mother would have to be away from Dillon for several long hours. Naturally the thought didn't sit well with her and she did not want to go as a result. Only after I volunteered to babysit him with my girlfriend, who was a dog lover and very nurturing, did she agree to go to the concert. I remember being left with a long list of step-by-step instructions, complete with hand-drawn illustrations, mapping out precisely how, when, and in what capacity the dog was to be fed, assisted outside, and put to bed that evening. It was extremely thorough, and I feared incurring my mother's wrath should I neglect to follow her instructions precisely and in a timely fashion. The night went without incident and Dillon was put to bed shortly before my parents returned late that night.

As fall approached, I remember my mind was filled with dread, as I knew that it was extremely unlikely that Dillon would or even could survive the coming winter. As September arrived, he was spending virtually all his time on his bed behind my mother's chair in the sunken living room, or on his bed in my parents' bedroom. His hindquarters were shriveled up and he could no longer control his bladder or his bowels. He required constant care and personal attention and couldn't be left alone for any reason now. He was wobbly on his feet and reached the point where he couldn't stand up by himself nor support himself without help once on his feet. The back of his thoracic harness had a handle that a person had to grab and pull on to help him onto his feet. Once up, the person had to continue to hold onto the handle to support him as he tried to walk. Sometimes he could manage a few steps unaided, but for the most part he needed constant assistance. His legs gave out more times than I care to remember, but he never fully gave up during those hard times.

The question became what to do with the beloved dog. I'm sure my parents had multiple private discussions on the matter, which most likely resulted in differing opinions. If I had to speculate (I was not privy to any of these discussions), I would say that my father recommended putting him down as soon as possible to spare him the pain and suffering he most assuredly was enduring. I would also speculate that my mother acknowledged that fact, and couldn't argue with that line of reasoning, but Dillon was her dog and she couldn't bring herself to just give up on him. I could see it in his eyes in those days. He was scared, and must have known the end was near, but he never gave up. There was something inherently alive inside of him that refused to die. There was a spark in his very soul that wanted to go on and resisted all attempts at being extinguished forever. It pained my heart to see him in such a sad state, but I drew courage from him as it became apparent that he was very unwilling to just curl up into a ball and wait for death. It was decided that no matter how painful or how exhausting it was, the family would not let Dillon go until *he* told us it was time. We would not just give up on him.

I was in my car when I got the phone call. Fortunately I was not far away from Auburn Street and I drove over as fast as I could. When I arrived I saw my father sitting in the back of my mother's SUV with Dillon. The hatchback was up and the dog was lying on his side and immobile. My father sat there solemnly and gently stroked Dillon's head. For a brief moment I feared he was gone, and a twinge of dread shot through my stomach like a bolt of lighting. As I approached the car I could see that he was still alive, but had finally given up.

"Your mother's inside trying to reach the vet. It's time," said my father with a tear in his eye. Dillon's veterinarian office was just down the street. It was literally in comfortable walking distance. However, on that day, his vet was unavailable and the best we could do was wait until tomorrow morning to take care of the unpleasant matter. My father and I carried Dillon back into the house and made him as comfortable as possible on his bed in my parents' bedroom. They explained to me that he had stopped eating and couldn't keep anything down including water. He had turned extremely sluggish and unresponsive. It was then that my mother knew that his time had come and that he was trying to tell her that it was okay—do what needed to be done.

I arrived back at Auburn Street early the next day. Dillon had had a bad night and I'm sure my mother stayed up with him for as long as her sleep-deprived mind would allow. She was lying on the floor next to him in the bedroom when I walked in. When the three of us finally got the courage to face the grisly task ahead, my father and I, like a couple of pallbearers, gently lifted Dillon up in a blanket and carried him to the car. All three of us then took the ten-second ride to the vet's office. His doctor was waiting for us and had Dillon brought inside on a stretcher. After quick examination, there was no hope for any form of miracle recovery and the decision was made to say our goodbyes then and there.

What happened next is one of the most painful and saddest memories I have to carry with me each and every day. My parents and I stayed with Dillon to the last. We watched as the vet administered the two shots that put Dillon to sleep. The first literally put him to sleep, while the second was the lethal dose that stopped his heart and officially ended his life. It was the first time any one of the three of us had witnessed the actual moment of death. (Both Mandy and Trucker were euthanized in the same manner, but I wasn't present at either time, and my parents, though responsible for delivering the dogs to the vet on those fateful days, did not witness the actual injections.) For the first time in my life, I saw the life of a cherished pet ebb away before my very eyes. I wish I could describe to you in detail how painful it is for me to recall and write this.

That was the end. Dillon died on a sunny day in early October 2014. He was thirteen years old. He was to be cremated and his ashes preserved, as was the tradition for our family's pets. My mother filled out the necessary paperwork among a sobbing veterinarian staff, and the three of us left to return to Auburn Street. The grief I was feeling was unrelenting and it was all I could do to keep from breaking down into a sobbing mess on the kitchen floor. There was little any of us wanted to say, and the overwhelming sadness and shock hadn't fully sunk in—that misery would come later. I had to return to work, and I knew my parents needed some privacy and time to themselves—particularly my mother.

That night I went to bed feeling as if I had lost my best friend. As fate would have it, I had an extremely remarkable and vivid dream that is as clear to me today as the night I dreamt it. In the dream I found myself standing in my parents' kitchen. I was alone and the sun was shining brightly outside. I went to the window and looked into the back yard. I saw nothing. No signs of man or beast. In the dream I wasn't sure what I was looking for, but I needed to find it, whatever it was. I walked from the kitchen out into the barren driveway. I looked upon Auburn Street and didn't see or hear a single car whiz by. It was eerily quiet. I remember slowly turning around and facing the front of the house. Something compelled me to kneel down. When my knee hit the pavement I heard a rapid "clacking" sound that was instantly recognizable. At that moment it became apparent whom I was searching for as a young, energetic, happy, and lovable Dillon raced around the corner of the house with his tongue out and his tail madly wagging. He jumped into my arms with as much love and admiration as I had ever known him to give. I hugged and patted that dog for what seemed like an eternity. Nothing made me feel happier than to see and hold him one last time. It was as if he was saying his personal, final goodbye to me in that dream. At that point, for some reason I knew everything was going to be okay. Dillon would always be with my family and me forever. I woke up in tears and I wasn't sure if they were tears of sadness or tears of joy. Dreams come and go, but that one will always remain in my heart and mind forever. Dillon was that special.

My family is blessed to have endless amounts of pictures and other tangible mementoes of Dillon. His memory is beautifully preserved in a stunning painting rendered by Burke Waldron's wife Janet, and even a few thoughtful, colorful, and very neatly done drawings created by my nephew Will. My father has also had Dillon's likeness captured by other artists and presented their work as a gift to my mother. I myself felt more should be done to preserve and honor Dillon's memory, so in 2015 I began scouring every picture file and video I possessed of that dog to create a video scrapbook of his life and everyone who was in it. I worked on it meticulously and finally got a finished product I was pleased with and one I felt the family would enjoy viewing as they remembered Dillon. It was simply titled *Remembering Dillon*. It was my main Christmas present to my mother that year.

The DVD was a hit. It was shown to the whole family that Christmas night. My mother was especially touched by it and viewed it privately several times after the initial showing. In time she started to email me the number of times she had watched it. I could only smile after receiving what seemed to be email after email after email from her. It was then that I realized just how much the gift meant to her, and it made me feel good knowing I had done something worthy of such high admiration. I should note that I had made a small tribute video to Trucker years earlier, but it was a much smaller and cruder production. Nevertheless, I think my mother's very grateful to have that video as well. There's very little video of Mandy in my archives, but one day I hope to get ambitious enough to scrape together everything I have of her and make her own little tribute DVD too.

Dillon is also immortalized in various elaborate scrapbooks created by my aunt and my mother herself. Both are scrapbooking enthusiasts and have put together many professional quality albums documenting his life and how he interacted with various family members—most prominently Will and Jack. It's also worth mentioning that my mother's close network of friends have also pitched in with numerous gifts and other forms of mementoes that will keep Dillon firmly in my mother's heart forever. As Mandy was our dog of the eighties, and Trucker the nineties, Dillon was our dog of the two thousands. He was one of a kind, and he was my pal.

As I write this now, Dillon has been gone for nearly two years. I think back to the days when he left us, and I realize that his passing had greater impact than I could have ever possibly imagined. For when Dillon died, an integral part of my family's very identity died with him—possibly forever. For what is a Morin household without a black Lab? From Mandy's arrival in 1978 to Dillon's demise in 2014, my parents had a black Lab under their roof. Over that span of thirty-six years, there were only two short periods when a dog wasn't present. From October 1993 through June of 1994—a period of eight months—and from September 2002 through December 2002—a period of just three months—mark the only times since 1978 that my parents were without a black Lab. So, for thirty-six years minus eleven months, my parents have never known their household to be barren of a four-legged friend.

My biggest fear was always centered around the impact the loneliness would have on my mother. She was the primary focal point in all three of the dog's lives. No one cared for them, spoiled them, or loved them more than she did. They became a regular part of her daily life, and to have that critical segment obliterated forever was somewhat inconceivable to me. I wasn't sure what the next step would be. She loved Dillon unquestionably, and he was perceived as irreplaceable. I wondered if my mother would test the waters yet again and seek out a new dog. The question has been brought up many times by many different and influential people in her life. The answer has always been no. In talking with both my parents about it, they claim that they are both too old and unfit to properly care for a new young dog. There's no question that if there was a new dog to enter their lives it would be a black Lab, but both feel the challenge of properly caring for the dog would be beyond their present capabilities—physically. That's fair, but if I were to venture my own speculation, I don't believe my parents are one hundred percent united in their decision. Deep inside I think my mother would go down the path of Lab ownership again if she were guaranteed another dog with similar appearance, obedience, and temperament as Dillon's. It is also my opinion that my father is firmly wedded to the belief that he and my mother are too old to handle a young dog and has no desire to be looking after an aging one in his early to mid eighties. I'm not sure he's keen on having a new dog even now.

So as things stand at this particular moment in time, there is no dog at the Morin residence on Auburn Street. I think my parents have adapted well, and though Dillon is still sorely missed, I don't think his absence is causing an all-consuming grief for them. I miss him too and still think of him regularly. A few years prior to Dillon's death, my brother's family acquired a dog of their own—only she wasn't a black Lab. In fact she was a small Boston Terrier named Anna. She's alive and well today and routinely visits the Morin household on Auburn Street whenever my brother and his family visit. So, in all honesty, the Morin household is not totally devoid of a canine presence.

I myself have been asked why I don't get a dog of my own—like a black Lab for instance. My reasoning is simple though could be construed as just a convenient excuse. I live alone in a small house in Portland. I have little room inside and a small yard outside. It's my belief that I could not give a new dog the proper space or attention it required to thrive. Dogs are like our children. They need supervision, affection, exercise, companionship, devotion, and most importantly, love. At this time in my life, I don't feel confident I could consistently provide all those things. However, if my life were to change and I were to get married, start a family, and move into a much bigger house, I wouldn't hesitate to introduce a black Lab into my new household. They are the perfect compliment to any family, and the ones I have had the pleasure of knowing all my life have enriched my existence in countless ways. Maybe someday…you just never know.

DILLON PHOTOGRAPHS

Dillon, posed for a formal picture as a young dog. Note the signature red collar.

Dillon celebrating his second birthday with a cake made especially for him.

Dillon and my mother celebrating her birthday together.

"Dill and Will." A special pair who grew up together.

Will getting ready to throw the "Air Dog" for his four-legged playmate.

On Mackworth Island. Dillon and Will enjoying a little outdoors adventure.

"Dill and Will" playing in their collapsed couch fort.

Two friends sharing a hug and a smile for the camera.

Dillon getting a "hand" from Jack.

Dillon performing for Jack. Notice the dog treat on his snout.

Dillon in the middle of the Auburn Street renovation. Notice the "Air Dog" in the background.

Dillon doing one of his patented "lip licks." Or maybe he's just sticking his tongue out at me!

Dillon charging into Highland Lake, one of his favorite places.

Even in winter, Dillon loved Highland Lake. Notice the ice by the water's edge.

Dillon posing for a picture at "The Dog Park."

Dillon posing with his favorite toy…the "Air Dog."

"The Lab Gang." Murphy, Dillon, and Bandit at "The Dog Park."

Dillon, a special dog who is sorely missed.

A "final" portrait of Dillon, drawn by Janet Waldron.

CHAPTER FOUR

MY REFLECTIONS

To try to accurately and completely sum up the total impact the three dogs mentioned in this book had on my life would be utterly futile and most likely require years of endless writing. Unfortunately I don't have that kind of time, so I'm now going to summarize my own personal thoughts and reflections as succinctly as I can. Each dog affected me differently and left its own personal and distinct mark on my life. But first, I suppose it's fitting to discuss some of the positive characteristics of black Labs in general.

Dogs enrich our lives in an endless variety of ways. I think that claim can be made for most pets—regardless of the species—but there's something inherently special and eternally bonding between humans and canines. There's no better example of that kind of close relationship than between a black Lab and its owner—in my humble opinion. Once a member of that special breed becomes a part of your world, you have a friend that shows you a form of undisputed devotion quite possibly unlike anything you have or will ever experience in your entire life. Relationships between men and women fail regularly and in extremely short periods of time; however, I have never known a Lab to ever stop loving its owner under any circumstances. They are fiercely loyal, unfailingly faithful, incredibly lovable, unbelievably tolerant, remarkably appreciative, and most always content regardless of whatever environment—pleasant or otherwise—they are in. They are also eternally optimistic and always seem to look to the bright side of any situation. In that sense, they are a very therapeutic animal with the ability to lift the spirits of even the most depressed individuals. Imagine a world not run by humans but by black Labs. War, intolerance, divisiveness, apathy, and possibly obesity would be wiped out over a very short time!

Black Labs don't talk back like disobedient children when scolded or disciplined. They don't complain when they don't get their way or are forced to go somewhere or do something they would prefer not to. They are grateful for the food they are fed and rarely stick their nose up, like a certain individual who wouldn't eat Hamburger Pie. They don't ask for much, and what they give in return is immeasurable. What kind of better scenario could a person wish for?

Dogs, in general, become a part of us. They're not just living objects that we possess; they're our companions, our helpers, our playmates, our therapists, our personal trainers, our guardians, and in many cases our children. It's easy to see why we humanize them like we do in this day and age. When they're happy, we're happy, and when they're in pain, we're in pain. They're not just animals relegated to the back yard or the house anymore. They ride with us in the car and escort us to most all of our daily activities and locations. They get on planes with us when we travel to distant lands and are rarely ever left out of our sight. They are, most assuredly, a quintessential and integral part of the goodness and purity in our lives.

No other place in the world can one witness the positive effects my family's three black Labs had on my mother than the house on Auburn Street. To walk inside is to see a treasure trove of black Lab memorabilia unlike most anything you've ever observed. Over the years, my mother has amassed a large collection of black-Lab-related objects and material that adorn virtually every room in the house. There are pictures and paintings that cover the walls, there are figurines and Lab-related novelties that enhance the shelves and countertops, there are Lab-shaped magnets of all sorts and varieties that cling to the fridge, and there are rugs designed in the likeness of black Labs spread out on the floors. As impressive as that seems, it is just the tip of the iceberg; for to try and describe *all* the black-Lab-related memorabilia placed throughout the house would be an exhausting exercise that would inevitably end in failure. However, there is one more special holiday symbol that should be mentioned as it relates to the family dogs. My parents' yearly Christmas tree, which I have the honor of decorating each December, is laden with black

Lab ornaments collected by or gifted to my mother over the years. It is an impressive sight and one worthy of all dog lovers.

It's interesting when I think back to all the pictures included in this book. Mandy's photographs were all taken with a standard 35mm camera (or a camera of that nature) and film. The majority of Trucker's images were captured by 35mm camera and film and instant Polaroid snapshots, but also with early and crude digital cameras. Dillon's pictures are almost entirely captured by advanced digital cameras or by smartphones. It's amazing to think of just how the world of photography evolved over the course of their lifetimes. All the images of Mandy and Trucker included in this book were harvested from dusty photo albums and an old shoebox filled with timeworn pet pictures. All of Dillon's images were collected from various computer hard drives—primarily my mother's.

I associate different objects with the three dogs. Let's start with Mandy first. It's important to restate for perspective that Mandy has been gone for twenty-three years as I now write this. Also, we must remember that she first came into my family's lives as far back as 1978. The world has noticeably changed a lot since then, but there are some small things that haven't. As pictured in this book, there are objects from Mandy's era that are still in my family's possession today. Most notably, those objects personify her wild and oftentimes destructive nature. The chewed up hammer and saw, the disfigured Lego and Star Wars toys, and even an old wooden stool laden with teeth marks are all originally preserved products from her era that pleasantly (and sometimes unpleasantly) remind us of who and what she was. I personally will do everything I can to make sure these objects remain in my family's possession for as long as possible. Why, you ask? Mandy was my family's first dog. She was the only true *family* dog. (Trucker and Dillon were my *mother's* dogs.) The things I have mentioned are the only tangible objects directly related to her. We grew up together and shared many memorable experiences (some mentioned earlier in her chapter) that remain with me to this day. To still have items that directly link to her past are not only important to me, but are also a testament to her enduring memory. She was an important member of our family. She lived the longest of all three of the dogs and she witnessed my growth from a small child to a young man. She left an indelible mark on me, and her stories will be told time and time again until everyone who knew her are gone.

I'm positive beyond a shadow of a doubt, that there are many others out there, friends and neighbors who I grew up with on Lester Drive who have their own special memories of our first dog. I'm sure if I ever have the pleasure of reconnecting with some of them who have moved on to distant places across the country, I'll be pleasantly surprised in hearing their personal stories and accounts of their memories of Mandy. There were of course other dogs that resided on Lester Drive, but I honestly think that Mandy was the most notorious and memorable. Someday someone may challenge me on that statement, but I'm not worried. I know that I have a very strong case.

Though Mandy lived over half her life on Auburn Street, I tend to always associate her with Lester Drive. I also think of her mainly in the times of my youth, probably because those were the days when she was young and healthy. Through all her problems and imperfections, she still had a profoundly positive impact on me. I am deeply grateful my parents didn't remove her from the family at the time when she had reached the apex of her unruliness. Though I was quite young in those days, that simple action taught me that one just can't give up on someone (or something) when times are at their worst and the future looks bleak. She was far from perfect, but she was all we had, and I couldn't imagine growing up without her. Having a dog at a young age is a wonderful training tool for new parents. Mandy may not have been the best or the brightest teacher, but she did impart some wisdom, and more importantly, love.

Trucker, unfortunately, had the least impact on my life, but there certainly are a few things worth mentioning. First I must remind the reader that of the three dogs written about here, Trucker was the one I was around the least. He was also in my mother's care for the shortest period of time. However, that's not to say that he didn't leave a favorable impression that I still find impactful today—he did.

Trucker showed me a side of a dog's intelligence that I had never seen or experienced before. His personality has always stuck out in my mind. He was one cool customer who always seemed to do things his way regardless of the consequences. Whether he was being disobedient or just downright silly, he did it in a style and flair that was his and his alone. He was adventurous, cunning, and full of surprises. He kept you on your toes and taught you never to underestimate him under any circumstances. His cleverness and ability to get what he wanted was quite remarkable and has left a lasting impression on me in the fourteen years he's been gone.

Despite his penchant for being rebellious and sniffing out trouble, true to his breed, he was extremely loyal and quite lovable. He took my mother to a whole new level of joy and provided her with a new dimension of happiness unlike anything I had ever seen before. He became *her* dog as their relationship blossomed and her maternal instincts were revived from dormancy. The love and companionship he provided was just what my mother needed at the time, as her two children were grown up and moving on to the next stage of their lives.

Trucker wasn't around for as long as we would have liked him to be, but I'm happy for the time he gave my family—especially my mother. He was a good dog and an excellent example of what to expect from a black Lab. His memory is alive and well on Auburn Street today, and every once in a while a story will come up in conversation that still leaves me shaking my head.

I think, in all honesty, of the three, Dillon probably was the most impactful and is probably the most sorely missed. The little road of happiness that Trucker built with my mother, was paved, widened, expanded, and turned into a superhighway of unparalleled love and admiration where Dillon was concerned. Of the three, I believe my mother cherished Dillon the most. He was her baby from the first day she discovered him until his demise. He was undisputedly *her* dog. Though Trucker lived with us longer than his Alaskan family, my mother was not his first owner. With Dillon it was different. Though he did come from a breeder, his first real taste of home and family came from his new mother—my mother.

To me, Dillon was just about everything you could want and every-thing you expected from a black Lab. He just seemed to be the perfect mix of all that is good in the breed. If I could pick and choose every characteris-tic and quality I wanted in a dog to construct my own personal family pet, I would start with Dillon's attributes. Sure, he had his own little quirky imperfections, but they actually made him more lovable. He was a big baby, spoiled and very coddled, but what he gave to my mother in return was well worth the price invested. Besides my two young nephews, Dillon was far and away the most important thing in my mother's life during his time on this earth.

The happiness he brought, the friendships he forged, and the generos-ity and goodwill he inspired are what I will always remember him for. One cannot enter my parents' home without immediately seeing some kind of re-minder of Dillon. His memory is on display the most throughout the house. There are more pictures, paintings, and mementoes of Dillon showcased than any other member of my family, with the possible exception of Jack and Will. (I have never taken the liberty to count them up and tally a score—it would simply take too long.)

Dillon's death hit me the hardest of the three, and there is rarely a day that goes by where I don't think of him in some capacity. My relationship with Dillon was unique because I knew him entirely as an adult, whereas I grew up with Mandy and I was just entering adulthood with Trucker. Dillon brought out feelings in me that adult men rarely show such as uncontrolled sadness just after his death. I miss him a lot, but I know there's someone else who misses him dearly every single day of her life—and you all know who that is.

Now I've reached the point where there's little else to say. I hope you've en-joyed reading this short book and have a better understanding of just how wonderful dog ownership—particularly black Lab ownership—can be. I hope you've also enjoyed some of the tales of my family's life I've imparted and can possibly relate some of them to your own family experiences. In closing, black Labrador retrievers are one of the most special breeds of dogs a family can possess. Seek them out, bring them into your own family, and let them into your heart. In the end you won't ever regret it! There are three that live in my heart to this day. Their names are Mandy, Trucker, and Dillon.

ACKNOWLEDGMENTS

My sincere thanks to all my friends and family, long past and present, who have provided me with inspiration and support throughout my life and have contributed to the development of this book through irreplaceable memories and photographs.

CHRISTOPHER MORIN was born, raised, and currently resides in Portland, Maine. He received a BA in Journalism from the University of Maine at Orono. He is a history enthusiast and has enjoyed creative writing ever since penning his first short story back in second grade. Along with this work of nonfiction, he is also the author of three fictional tales titled *A Tale of Life & War*, *The Besieged*, and *The Rebel's Wrath*.